SCRAPBOOK pages
starring your BABY

bryce
in the
BUCKET

MEMORY MAKERS BOOKS

Executive Editor Kerry Arquette   *Founder* Michele Gerbrandt

Art Director Andrea Zocchi

Designer Nick Nyffeler

Art Acquisitions Editor Janetta Abucejo Wieneke

Craft Editor Jodi Amidei

Photographer Ken Trujillo

Contributing Photographers Brenda Martinez, Terry Ownby, Jennifer Reeves

Cover Photo Stylist Sylvie Abecassis

Contributing Writer Kelly Angard

Editorial Support Karen Cain, Emily Curry Hitchingman, MaryJo Regier, Lydia Rueger, Dena Twinem

Contributing Memory Makers Masters Joanna Bolick, Jennifer Bourgeault, Susan Cyrus, Brandi Ginn, Diana Hudson, Torrey Miller, Michelle Pesce, Denise Tucker, Andrea Lyn Vetten-Marley

Memory Makers® *Scrapbook Pages Starring Your Baby*

Published by Memory Makers Books, an imprint of F+W Publications, Inc.

4700 East Galbraith Road, Cincinnati, OH 45236

First edition. Printed in China.

11 10 09 08 07   7 6 5 4 3

Library of Congress in Publication Data

Memory Makers Books, © 2004

Scrapbook pages starring your baby

p. cm.

Includes index

ISBN-13: 978-1-892127-45-7 (pbk. : alk. paper)

ISBN-10: 1-892127-45-8 (pbk. : alk. paper)

1. Photograph albums 2. Photographs—Conservation and restoration
3. Scrapbooks 4. Babybooks I. Title

TR465.S39347 2004

745.593—dc22

Memory Makers Books is the home of *Memory Makers*, the scrapbook magazine dedicated to educating and inspiring scrapbookers.

Visit us on the Internet at www.memorymakers.com

THIS BOOK BELONGS TO

All the world's a stage,
And all the men and women merely players:
They have their exits and their entrances;
And one man in his time plays many parts...

"As You Like It" - William Shakespeare

Table of Contents

7   Introduction

8   Scrapbook Tools and Supplies

10   Creating a Scrapbook Page

A Star is Born 12-37

A baby makes an entrance to an already-adoring audience that waits, captivated, to hear the newcomer's first cry and applaud his first ootch and coo. Whether awake or sleeping, an infant is center stage, and you, who loves him most, will inevitably spotlight him in memorable photos preserved on stellar scrapbook pages.

Move In For a Close-Up 38-59

That baby face is even cuter up close-and-personal. Star quality registers in every dimple and eye twinkle. Whether captured in formal portraits or snapshots, babies absolutely know how to fill a frame. Scrapbook those close-up photos of your child's first head shots and intimate photo moments on pages that are worthy of standing ovations.

Lights, Camera, ACTION! 60-81

You don't need to shoot moving pictures to capture your baby's wiggles, tottering steps, wobbly self-feedings and exploration of the world. These and other on-the-go moments in your little star's life make great still photos as well. Record them on four-thumbs-up pages that vibrate with energy and enthusiasm.

Let's Shoot Some Black-and-White 82-103

Everything old is new again, and the popularity of technicolor snapshots has swung full circle for many scrapbookers who are discovering the benefits of capturing their babies in timelessly classy black-and-white. Dress up the pages in glamorous colors or keep the focus on the leading player with monochromatic papers and embellishments.

The Supporting Cast 104-125

Applause. The star is taking a bow, and friends and family are cheering. Roll out the red carpet and scrapbook photos of your baby interacting with fans. Whether at home or out on the town, your baby was meant to shine. Capture those special sharing moments on terrific pages that are as one-of-a-kind as a premiere opening.

126 Additional Art Instructions

127 Sources

128 Index

Fresh from God's cradle and into my arms,
My daughter was wrapped in a blanket of love.
This tiniest package of heart wrenching charms
Was sent on a mission by angels above,
To snatch up my heart and to make it her own –
A young mother's heart that had barely been worn
She needn't have bothered, for truth to be known...
I gave it to her long before she was born.

Introduction

A star is born…a special little shining light. And from that moment on, your life will never be the same. It has been said that when a child enters the world, a parent is born. How true. Your child naturally becomes the center of attention, the focal point of all activity. At family gatherings the little newcomer is passed from grandparent to aunt to uncle. Every coo and smile is reason for applause from the enamored audience. And their infatuation doesn't falter as the baby progresses through all those important "firsts"—first cereal, first roll-over, first unsupported sitting session. And there you are, capturing it all with your camera.

Photos of your baby are perhaps the most precious you'll ever take. They are made more so because each and every moment you've recorded is one-of-a-kind. There is no baby like your own, and the experiences you share are unique to the special bond between you. It is nothing short of a labor of love to preserve your baby's pictures in an album that will protect the photos and on layouts that will underscore their importance.

In Scrapbook Pages Starring Your Baby you'll find hundreds of ideas for creating beautiful baby-themed layouts on more than a hundred scrapbook pages. Discover beautiful borders, backgrounds, title treatments and embellishments that you can use on your own page designs. Whether you're scrapbooking formal portraits or more candid shots of your child's daily activities, you're sure to find page ideas that get your creative juices flowing. You'll also find cutting-edge ideas for scrapbooking your favorite black-and-white photos.

Included in Scrapbook Pages Starring Your Baby are title ideas, photo tips, checklists, journaling concepts, reader's memories and a bit of trivia as well as great concepts for preserving memorabilia—locks of your baby's first haircut, birth certificates and hospital bracelets—in your album.

If this is your first venture into creative scrapbooking, it will almost certainly not be your last. There is something uniquely fulfilling about creating scrapbook pages for your children. In years to come, long after your child has left diapers and bibs behind, you'll find yourselves enjoying your child's baby album together. The stories behind the pictures will flow and already-strong bonds will be strengthened.

Even though my children are now tweens and teens, they will always be stars to me, and I will continue to record and capture their personalities, milestones and achievements in my scrapbooks. I wish for you the same.

Michele

Michele Gerbrandt
Founding Editor
Memory Makers magazine

Basic Scrapbook Tools and Supplies

Every artist, from cinematographer to sculptor, painter to musician needs the right tools and supplies in order to create.
Scrapbook artists are no exception. Before you begin scrapbooking your baby take a trip to your local scrapbook or craft store, or
visit one of the many suppliers of scrapbook supplies online. You'll want to stock up on the basics and a wealth of wonderful materials that will
result in award-winning scrapbook pages.

Albums

Albums are sold in a variety of styles including post-bound, strap-hinge, three-ring binder and spiral as well as a variety of sizes from 4 x 6" to 12 x 15". Choose one that best suits your shelf space and works well with your personal scrapbooking style.

Paper

Paper is available in solid cardstock and in hundreds of festive and artistic patterns and also as speciality papers including vellum, suede, mulberry, handmade paper and metallics. Paper is used for backgrounds, matting, page elements such as journaling blocks and borders as well as design additions.

Pens and Markers

From fine-point to large brush styles, these tools are used in journaling as well as for adding decorative flourishes to page design. Chose writing tools that are safe for scrapbooking. Practice using your writing tool on scrap paper before attempting to write directly on your scrapbook page.

Adhesives

Modern scrapbook adhesives insure strong binding of photos, memorabilia and embellishments to scrapbook papers without damaging photos or memorabilia. They are available in a variety of forms including glue pens and sticks, photo splits and tape runners. Some varieties offer permanent bonding and others allow you to remove your photos at a later date.

Cutting Tools

Decorative scissors, paper trimmers, craft knives, punches and shape cutters are used to create decorative mats, journaling and title blocks as well as crop photos and create decorate page elements. Whether cutting straight edges, curving corners or creating whimsical shapes, there is a cutting tool for every job.

Stickers, Stamps and Templates

Available in countless designs and patterns that suit almost every page theme, these tools are used to add decorative designs and shapes to your scrapbook pages. Emboss over their design, color within their borders, use them as guidelines for journaling. The opportunities are endless.

Embellishments

Tags, beads, fibers, charms and other adornments are used to decorate and add flair to scrapbook pages. Combine them or use them alone for customized decorating.

Create a Layout

The scrapbook page is your big screen and you are the director who gets to determine the mood, balance and content of your presentation. There are no hard-and-fast rules when it comes to the creation of a scrapbook page, however many strong layouts build on common themes and design principals.

Create a Layout

Focal Point

Choose an enlarged, matted, unique or exceptional photo for your page's primary focal point. The goal is not only to capture the viewer's attention, but also to visually ground your layout. All surrounding photos should support this central image.

Balance

Place your photos on a one- or two-page layouts. Note that very large, bright or busy photos may dominate the page and need to be balanced by less busy counterparts. Move the photos around until you've achieved a look that is visually appealing. Remember to leave space for a page title, journaling and embellishments.

Color

Choose a background, mat papers and design additions that complement your photos. Consider pulling colors found in the pictures themselves, or select colors that help reinforce your page theme. When it comes to color, less is often more, so be selective in your choices and don't let the colors on the page overwhelm the photos.

Crop and Assemble

Cropping

Photo cropping can remove a busy background from a picture or reduce the image to a workable size or more interesting shape. Never crop one-of-a-kind photos. Work on duplicates.

Matting

Photo mats provide an island for your pictures which grounds them and draws the viewer's eye, adding visual balance and contrast. Photo mats serve as a buffer between memorabilia that is potentially damaging and pictures. Photo mats can be cut in decorative shapes, can be layered or embellished.

Mounting

Photos, memorabilia, journaling and title blocks are mounted on scrapbook pages with archivally safe adhesives. You may also wish to use photo corners to mount your materials. These corners are adhered to the background paper of a page and the corners of photo mats are inserted, allowing the photos to be removed at a later date, if desired.

Title and Journaling

A creative title announces the theme of your scrapbook page and journaling is a way of recording the details surrounding the page. Journaling often cites the date the photos were taken, those appearing in the pictures and information about the event. It may be done as bullets, quotes, sayings, poems or a personal reflection. Write directly on your scrapbook page or create title or journaling blocks and mount them in your album.

Embellish

Much of the fun in the creation of a scrapbook layout is in the embellishing. Whether you wish to decorate your page with ribbon, fiber or punched paper shapes, stickers, beads, charms, tiny metal frames or other ephemera, you'll find that dressing up your page provides the finishing touch.

The Completed Page

The completed page brings together all your elements in an artistic and emotional display of images and words. It tells a story about a person or an event in a way that you and your ancestors will be able to relate to in decades to come. It is testimony to your talent and to your caring.

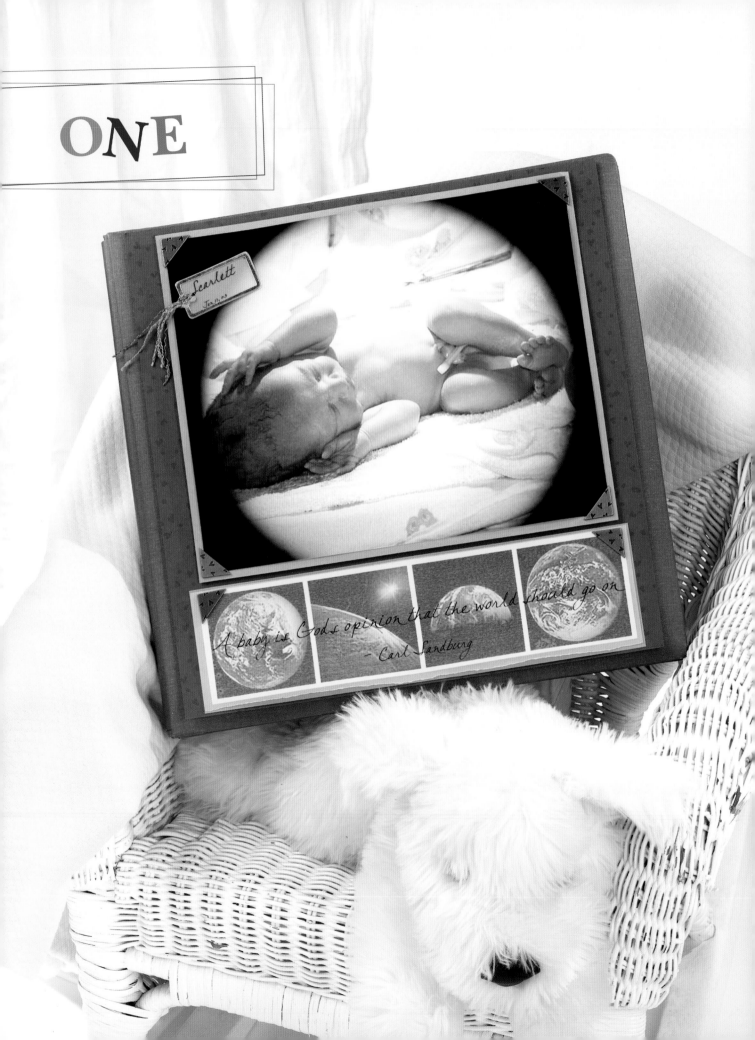

A Star is Born

From the heavens a child arrives, and your life is changed forever. A baby becomes the center of your own personal universe. You find yourself pausing in the middle of a sentence—holding your breath until your ears catch the sound of that tiny sigh from the cradle across the room, burying your nose in the delicious folds at the base of your baby's neck to inhale newborn sweetness, running your fingers over tiny toenails and looking for stardust in your child's eyes. The birth of your baby and the months that follow are distilled magic. And although you believed that you couldn't love your baby any harder, you become aware that your love is growing with the rapid and regular pace of your baby's heartbeat. Scrapbook the miracle of these early days, weeks and months in your baby's life on pages as pure as your child and as powerful as your feelings.

God makes stars. I just produce them.
Samuel Goldwyn

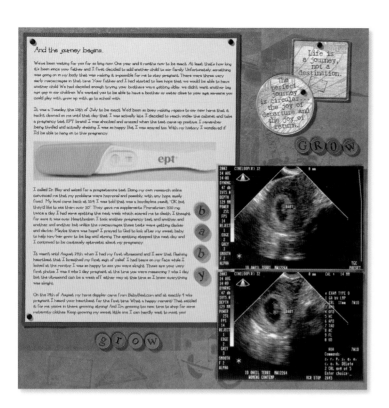

Grow Baby Grow

A scanned pregnancy test strip and ultrasound photos commemorate Terrilyn's success in becoming pregnant. Print journaling with pregnancy strip image on tan cardstock; mat on rust cardstock. Attach to patterned background cardstock with brads. Scan and print ultrasound photos; layer on page. Attach metal title letter eyelets on journaling block and background cardstock. Adhere quote stickers on metal-rimmed tags; attach to page with brads.

Terrilyn O'Neil, Fort Myers, Florida

Supplies: Patterned cardstock, quote stickers/Club Scrap; metal letter eyelets, metal-rimmed tags/Making Memories; tan and rust cardstocks; brown brads

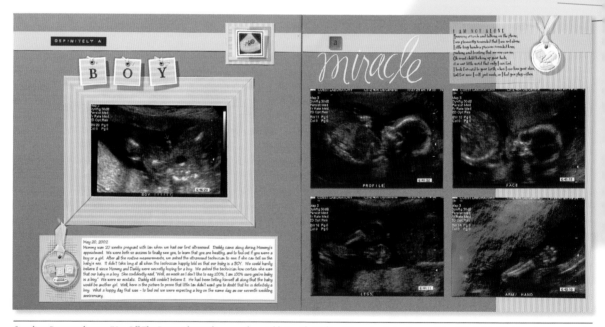

Supplies: Patterned paper/Hot Off The Press; white rub-on word, metal letter tile/Making Memories; baby theme sticker/Me & My Big Ideas; letter stamps/ (source unknown); green and white cardstocks; vellum; buttons; mesh; eyelets; embroidery floss; tape label; metal-rimmed tags; ribbon; square and circle punches; black ink

Definitely a Boy

Valerie preserved delicate ultrasound photos by scanning the originals and printing the images on photo paper. Slice a 4" strip of patterned paper; mount at right side of right-hand page. Slice two narrow strips of green cardstock; horizontally mount near top of both pages. Mount four photos on right page. Transfer white word rub-on above photo; mount metal letter on green strip. Print poem on vellum; cut to size and mount at top of page with embellished tag tied with ribbon. Slice patterned paper into four strips for photo frame on left page, angling corners. Mount over photo. Print journaling on cardstock; mat. Punch circle from patterned paper to fit inside metal-rimmed tag; punch small hole at top and tie with ribbon. Mount dimensional baby-themed items on tag; layer over yellow mesh on journaling mat. Punch three 1" and 1¼" squares from patterned and white papers. Layer squares; stamp letters. Attach eyelets in each layered square; tie with embroidery floss. Mount at top of framed photo with foam spacers. Using a label-maker, punch letters into label strip; mount on green strip. Adhere ultrasound sticker on white cardstock; crop and mount on matted patterned paper with foam spacer.

Valerie Salmon, Carmel, Indiana

New Life

Maria features elegant patterned paper to celebrate the exciting months of pregnancy. Tie ribbon around brown cardstock strip; mount on patterned paper background with sanded edges. Mount photos; layer one over patterned paper with sanded edges. Adhere dimensional letters on page and walnut ink-stained tag for title; tie with ribbon. Mount metal bookplate over photo caption printed on brown cardstock. Stamp date at bottom of page.

Maria Newport, Smyrna, Georgia

Supplies: Patterned paper/Karen Foster Design; dimensional letters/ Creative Imaginations; walnut ink-stained tag; brown cardstock; ribbon; metal bookplate; sandpaper; ink

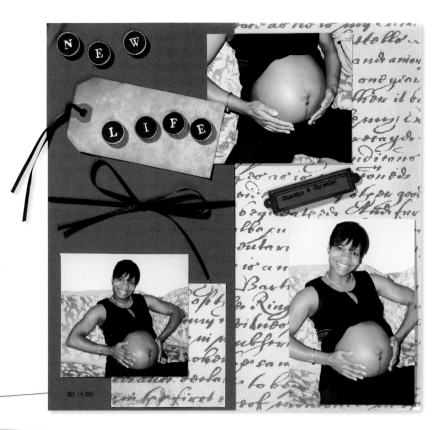

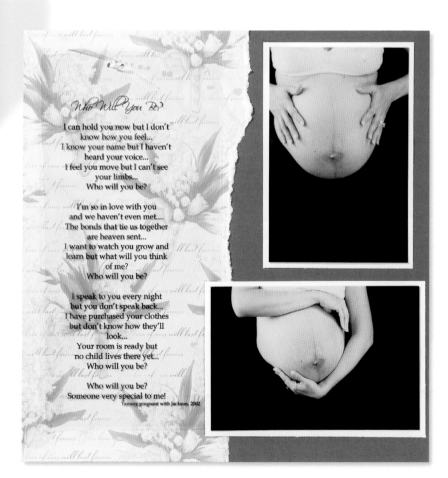

Who Will You Be?

Kate expresses a mother's thoughts and dreams as she awaits her baby's birth through an original poem. Tear patterned paper to fit half of green background cardstock; mount on left side of cardstock. Mat photos on white cardstock. Print title and journaling on transparency; cut and layer over patterned paper. Punch holes near top of layered papers; tie with ribbon.

Kate Nelson, Fountain, Colorado

Supplies: Patterned paper/Paper Adventures; green and white cardstocks; transparency; yellow ribbon

Connor's Room

Jennifer documents the anticipation of a baby with this colorful jungle-themed nursery. Print journaling on yellow cardstock; add chalk highlights. Ink edges of yellow background cardstocks. Slice two strips of green cardstock; mount at top and bottom of left page. Adhere tree branch and leaf stickers at inside edges of strips. Print title on blue cardstock; silhouette cut letters and mount over tree branch sticker. Single and double mat photos for left page on brown and blue cardstocks; rub white ink around edges of brown mat. Divide right page into nine equal segments; crop photos and colored cardstock to fit segments. Adhere animal stickers on colored cardstock squares; rub edges with white ink; mount. Tie buttons with twine; mount at corners of center square.

Jennifer Bourgeault, Macomb Township, Michigan

It took a few months to decide on a theme for your nursery. Daddy wanted a sports theme and Mommy wanted more of a baby theme. Well, after numerous trips to Babies 'R' Us & The Baby's Room we finally agreed on a jungle theme! Daddy and Grandpa Potapa painted, wallpapered and hung the border just in time for the baby shower. Mommy would hang out in your room for hours just imagining what life was going to be like when our precious little guy arrived!

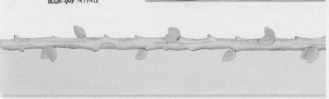

Supplies: Jungle-themed stickers/Doodlebug Design; yellow, blue, brown and green cardstocks; white ink; buttons; twine; chalk

MEMORABILIA CHECKLIST

A scrapbook is the perfect place to keep memorabilia collected during your pregnancy and your baby's early days. Be sure to hold on to the following:

- ❑ Positive pregnancy test
- ❑ Ultrasound photos
- ❑ Shower invitations and cards
- ❑ Pieces of wrapping paper from baby gifts
- ❑ Gift list and registry
- ❑ Hospital bracelets, bassinet name tag
- ❑ Hospital and doctor bills
- ❑ Copy of doctor's notes
- ❑ Copy of birth certificate

- ❑ Foot- and handprints
- ❑ Birth announcement
- ❑ News and bulletin announcements
- ❑ Congratulations cards and letters
- ❑ Religious ceremony mementos
- ❑ Formula, food and diaper labels
- ❑ Growth, development and inoculation records
- ❑ Lock of hair from first haircut

Making a Room for Baby

Show details of a baby's room with a photo-blocked layout. Crop photos into squares and rectangles of equal height or width; mount on white cardstock, leaving room between each photo. Mat small assembled photo block on red cardstock before mounting at bottom of left page. Print title and journaling on white cardstock; crop and mount on page. Tie ribbon and mount between title and journaling; adhere letter pebble in title. Double mat large photo on white and blue cardstocks; cut to fit next to title/journaling block. Mat large photo block on right page with blue cardstock before mounting on tan background cardstock. Stamp date on green and yellow cardstock strips; mount with heart brads.

Jennifer Miller, Humble, Texas

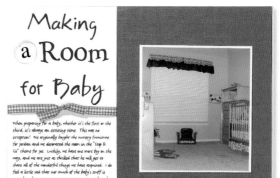

Supplies: Letter pebble/Creative Imaginations; date stamp/ Making Memories; heart brads/Provo Craft; white, red, blue, tan, green and yellow cardstocks; red gingham ribbon

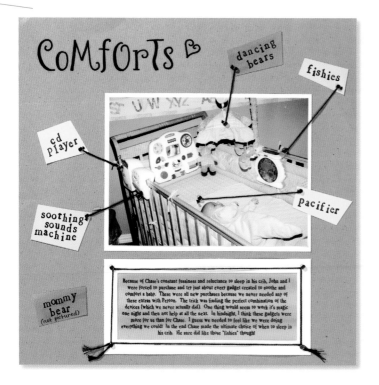

Comforts

Amy maintains a sense of humor at the gadgets she purchased to comfort her fussy baby. Stamp words on yellow, green and blue cardstocks for labels; chalk green cardstock. Cut into angled shapes; mount around photo matted on white cardstock. Attach brads on labels and corresponding items in photo; string embroidery floss from brads on labels to brads on photos. Print journaling on patterned vellum; layer behind frame sliced from white cardstock. Mount brads on corners; wrap embroidery floss around frame and secure under brads. Adhere letter title stickers.

Amy Warren, Tyler, Texas

Supplies: Patterned vellum/Worldwin; letter stickers/Doodlebug Design; letter stamps/PSX Design; yellow, green, white and blue cardstocks; black embroidery floss; brads; ink; chalk

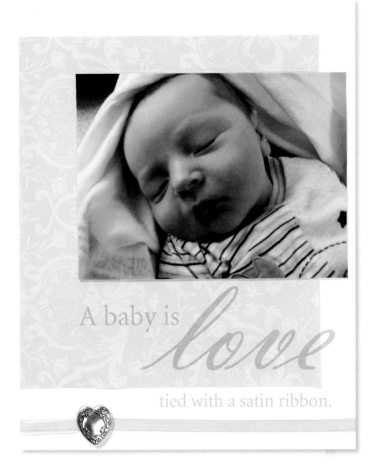

A baby is *love* tied with a satin ribbon.

A Baby Is Love

Susan converted a portrait of her newborn baby to a duo-tone with photo-editing software. Mount patterned paper piece on cream background cardstock. Print title before mounting photo. Mount blue ribbon at bottom of page and embellish with heart charm.

Susan Cyrus, Broken Arrow, Oklahoma

Supplies: Patterned paper/Anna Griffin; silver heart charm/Boutique Trims; cream cardstock; blue ribbon

BABY NAMING TIPS

Selecting a baby name is an exciting responsibility. Take care to select the name that is just right for your child.

- Remember that your baby will carry the chosen name throughout his life. What may be cute for a child may not be as "cute" for an adult. Pick a name that your child will feel comfortable with across the decades.

- Select a name that is largely "taunt-resistant."

- Think about the meaning of the name. A lovely definition can make a chosen name even more special.

- Listen to how the name fits with your last name. Too many syllables, repetitive consonants and such can make a name difficult to say.

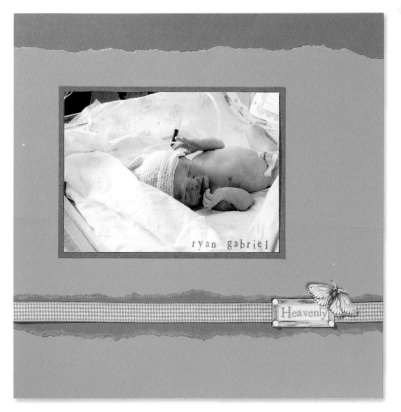

ryan gabriel

Heavenly

Heavenly

Corina uses a single image to parallel the birth of her son to that of a butterfly emerging from its cocoon. Layer torn cardstock strips on background cardstock. Wrap ribbon across page over torn strip. Mount bookplate over title stamped on vellum; attach with brads. Adhere butterfly sticker. Stamp name on photo; mat on gray metallic cardstock and mount on page.

Corina Minkoff, Cedar Grove, New Jersey

Supplies: Metallic cardstock/Bazzill; letter stamps/PSX Design; butterfly sticker/Magenta; bookplate/www.twopeasinabucket.com; blue cardstock; vellum; ribbon; white brads; ink

While You Were Sleeping

Susan pieced together a large title word using photo-editing software. Lay out title on scanned enlarged image in computer program; print and trim to desired size. Print same title on white cardstock; cut to size. Layer photo with partial title over white cardstock with title, making sure to line up title letters. Achieve this same look with large silhouette-cut letters layered on an enlarged photo and background. Mount two photos at bottom of page. Slice a strip of patterned paper to fit open space next to enlarged photo. Stamp sentiment on patterned paper. String star charms on ribbon; secure to page. Wrap ribbon ends over top of page and secure.

Susan Cyrus, Broken Arrow, Oklahoma

Supplies: Patterned paper/Bo-Bunny Press; letter stamps/Hero Arts; star charms/Boutique Trims; white cardstock; satin ribbon; black ink

April Showers

Susan's son peeks out from a snugly refuge on a rainy day. Print title and journaling on background patterned paper. Mount photo near top of page. Tie a jump ring to ribbon; mount under photo; wrap ribbon around edges of page and secure. Attach charm to jump ring and secure. Mount paint chip strip at left side of page. Adhere orange and blue dimensional flower stickers.

Susan Cyrus, Broken Arrow, Oklahoma

Supplies: Patterned paper/Colorbök; silver umbrella charm/Card Connection; flower stickers/EK Success; paint chip strip; white satin ribbon; silver jump ring

Display of Documents

The birth of a baby generates treasured documents including birth announcements, hospital records and thank-you notes. Incorporate these items on spectacular scrapbook pages to preserve them for generations. Take a look at these eight special scrapbook layouts (pages 20-24) designed to open your eyes to the many ways you can include memorabilia on your baby spreads.

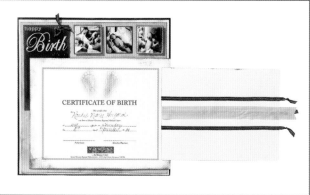

Happy Birth Day

Kelly superimposes text on an enlarged photo for the cover of a hinged page element that lifts to reveal the hospital certificate, photos and journaling. Double mat pink patterned paper with ivory and black cardstocks for background; ink edges. Scan birth certificate and print on transparency; layer over large photo. Cut three pieces of gingham ribbon and one piece of pink ribbon into 13" lengths; knot gingham ribbons at one end. Mount one piece of gingham ribbon on pink ribbon. Mount ribbon strips across back of layered photo, extending ribbons beyond right edge. Center layered photo with ribbons over birth certificate. Adhere length of ribbon that lays on the birth certificate. Make a hinge to attach birth certificate to page from a 1½ x 8½" strip of black cardstock. Score lengthwise and fold. Mount outside left panel of folded hinge to back of certificate, lining up folded edge with certificate edge. Mount. Slide inside left panel of folded hinge behind right side of cardstock background; mount. Wrap ribbon ends around edge of background cardstock and secure. Adhere silver letter stickers at top of black cardstock strip; tear right edge and ink. Print one title word on pink cardstock; silhouette cut. Mount typewriter letters with foam spacers. Tie gingham ribbon to silver heart charm and mount near title. Single and double mat photos on ivory and black cardstocks; ink photo and matting edges. Print journaling and scanned footprints on transparency. Layer all on page with foam spacers, mounting two photos along the top of page.

Kelly Angard, Highlands Ranch, Colorado

Supplies: Patterned paper/Karen Foster Design; letter stickers/All My Memories/Making Memories; heart charm/Boxer Scrapbook Productions; ivory, pink and black cardstocks; transparency; gingham and pink ribbon; metallic rub-ons, black, pink and silver inks

Announcing Jared

Jennifer preserves her son's printed birth announcement by mounting it on patterned background paper. Adhere sticker letters under announcement. Layer preprinted alphabet dots in conchos; attach to page.

Jennifer Miller, Humble, Texas

Supplies: Patterned paper/Chatterbox; letter stickers/Creative Imaginations; alphadots, conchos/Scrapworks

Brinley Nicole Ginn

Brandi announces the arrival of her baby with feminine details. Tear a narrow strip of patterned paper; vertically mount at right side of patterned background paper. Print birth information on vellum; crop and layer over matted photo. Punch two small holes at top of layered announcement; tie with ribbon. Double mat bottom photo on white and black cardstocks. Mount metal frames over small photos; adhere over torn patterned paper strip.

Brandi Ginn, Lafayette, Colorado

Supplies: Patterned paper/Magenta; metal frames/Making Memories; white and black cardstocks; vellum; sheer pink ribbon

Love

Cori stitches an embellished pocket to store her daughter's birth certificate. Cut colored cardstock to fit color-blocked sections; mount on cardstock background. Stitch along seams of colored cardstock. Brush pink acrylic paint on large plastic frame and metal-rimmed tag; dry. Rub on letter/word transfers on card-stock, metal-rimmed tag and large frame. Stitch button on metal-rimmed tag with embroidery floss; mount on torn card-stock strip. Stitch to page along top and bottom of cardstock strip with embroidery floss; slide birth certificate behind stitched strip. Mount frame over cropped photos. Embellish frame and page with layered metal and die-cut vellum flowers and stitched button. Journal on vellum; layer under stitched buttons.

Cori Dahmen, Portland, Oregon

Supplies: Rub-on letters, metal flower/Making Memories; large plastic photo frame/Jest Charming; pink cardstock; vellum; metal-rimmed tag; embroidery floss; buttons; pink acrylic paint

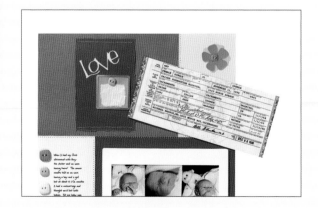

Congratulations

Polly organized a dangling display of small gift cards on top of a vellum pocket stuffed with notes celebrating her son's birth. Tear a strip of light green cardstock; mount near top of green cardstock background. Tear bottom edge of white tag; adhere letter sticker and tie with ribbon. Stamp remainder of title word; mount buttons. Mount green and white trim and green netting near top of page. Diagonally cut a 7½" vellum square with scalloped edges. Apply adhesive along left and bottom edges of vellum and mount to create pocket. Attach eyelets at corners and string with fiber. Insert cards in pocket. Tear photo edges; embellish with fibers and buttons and mount on pocket. Assemble birth information on yellow cardstock: mount letter beads; stamp name. Stamp month and year; adhere date number stickers. Mount frames with foam spacers. Loop ribbon over green netting strip and tie bow; mount framed birth information over bottom of ribbon. Attach cards to bow with metal chain. Wrap corners of page with ribbon.

Polly McMillan, Bullhead City, Arizona

Supplies: Letter sticker/Me & My Big Ideas; letter stamps/Hero Arts; letter beads, date stamp/Making Memories; metal frames/Magic Scraps; light green, green and yellow cardstocks; vellum; tag; blue gingham ribbon; fibers; green/white fabric trim; green and blue buttons; green coastal netting; eyelets; black ink

Our Baby Girl

A treasured family quilt inspired the patchwork design Diana used to display "best wishes." Scan and reduce sentiments from congratulations cards; print on pink cardstock. Punch sentiments and patterned papers into squares. Sponge with brown aging ink; distress edges. Mount squares on brown cardstock background. Mat photo on pink cardstock; stitch around matting. Age and distress mat. Cut patterned paper to fit inside oval metal-rimmed tag; punch holes at both ends. Tie ribbon at one end; string loose end through holes behind tag and wrap across photo. Secure behind matted photo. Die cut letters from brown cardstock; mount on tag.

Diana Hudson, Bakersfield, California

Supplies: Patterned papers/Daisy D's/EK Success/Paper Adventures; die-cut letters/QuicKutz; date stamp, metal-rimmed tag/Making Memories; pink and brown cardstocks; square punch; brown aging ink; green ribbon

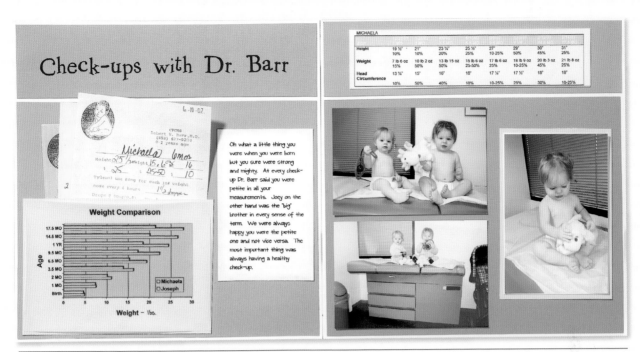

MICHAELA								
Height	19½"	21"	23¼"	25½"	27"	29"	30"	31"
	10%	10%	20%	25%	10-25%	25%	45%	25%
Weight	7 lb 6 oz	10 lb 2 oz	13 lb 15 oz	15 lb 6 oz	17 lb 6 oz	18 lb 9 oz	20 lb 3 oz	21 lb 8 oz
	15%	50%	50%	50%	25%	25%	45%	25%
Head Circumference	13¾"	15"	16"	16"	17¼"	17½"	18"	18"
	10%	50%	40%	10%	10-25%	25%	30%	10-25%

Supplies: Gray, blue and white cardstocks; vellum; chalk

Checkups With Dr. Barr

Tracy organizes her twins' first year of growth information with easy-to-read charts. Mount gray and blue cardstocks on white cardstock background. Print title on gray cardstock; mount as title border. Journal on white cardstock; chalk edges. Print graph and chart on vellum; layer over pink and white cardstocks. Mount graph on pink cardstock as a pocket; adhere along sides and bottom only. Slip doctor's information sheets behind pocket. Double mat focal photo. Mount second chart, additional photos and focal photo on right page.

Tracy A. Weinzapfel Burgos, Ramona, California

Certificate of Baptism

Jeniece accentuates the sanctity of a blessed event with transferred images and religious symbols layered among lace. Tear edges of blue cardstock; chalk. Mat on white cardstock; apply silver metallic rub-ons around cardstock edge. Stamp large fleur-de-lis design on blue cardstock with acrylic paint. Brush paint along bottom of cardstock to highlight journaling; dry. Print journaling on transparency; mount over painted area. Scan baptism certificate and photo; print on iron-on transfer paper made for inkjet printers. Transfer images onto cotton fabric according to manufacturer's directions. Stitch lace trim around edges of fabric certificate. Mount pieces of lace along right side of blue cardstock. Layer fabric photo over lace; embellish with satin bow and guardian angel medal. Wrap lace from lower left corner up over bottom of fabric photo; wrap around edges of page; secure. Stitch around entire page along torn edges of blue cardstock. Attach rosary beads at top of fabric certificate with diaper pin. Secure beads and cross on page.

Jeniece Higgins, Lake Forest, Illinois

Supplies: Fleur-de-lis stamp/Plaid; blue and white cardstocks; blue chalk; metallic rub-ons; white acrylic paint; transparency; lace; diaper pin; rosary beads; cross; guardian angel medal; ribbon; cotton fabric; iron-on transfer paper

Supplies: Patterned paper/SEI; letter stamps/PSX Design; slide mounts/Composite Crafts

Chase

Melinda's love for every part of her son multiplied after he melted her heart with his first smile. Affix slide mounts over cropped photos; mount all photos on patterned cardstock background. Stamp title and text on page.

Melinda Adams, Wantirna, Victoria, Australia

Lucy

Bethany's combination of feminine papers and bold graphic lines adds sugar and spice to a baby girl's layout. Mat photo on patterned paper; layer over white patterned paper strip matted with black cardstock on pink patterned paper background. Wrap bottom of white patterned paper strip with pink and black fibers. Layer torn patterned paper on tag and wrap with pink fiber; dangle charm with wire. Stamp name and date. Adhere letter sticker on brad; attach over black punched circle.

Bethany Fields, Amarillo, Texas
Photo: René Brown, Adrian, Texas

Supplies: Patterned papers/7 Gypsies/K & Co./Me & My Big Ideas; letter sticker/Creative Imaginations; letter stamps/Hero Arts; charm/ Doodlebug Design; black cardstock; pink and black fibers; silver brad; circle punch

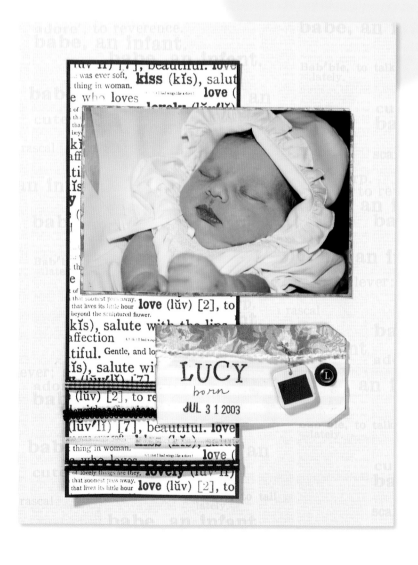

I Knew I Loved You

Mary's pastel baby page is as soft as a lullaby. Adhere striped patterned strip on pink patterned background paper; attach ribbon across upper edge of strip. Stitch second block of patterned paper to overlap striped strip and third piece of patterned paper across first two paper pieces. Create photo corners with scrap lace. Adhere photo to page. Adhere circle tag embellished with fibers and title. Add title letter stickers and journal. Finish with "You" words machine embroidered on mulberry paper. Mount on page.

Mary Zimmer, New Baltimore, Michigan

Supplies: Patterned paper/KI Memories/7Gypsies; vellum letters/Creative Imaginations; letter stamps/Stampin'Up!; mulberry paper; fibers; lace; ink

Supplies: Patterned papers/Hot Off The Press/K & Co.; yellow cardstock; mulberry paper; pink vellum; brads; embroidery floss; paper yarn; buttons; fiber; paper clip; beads; wire; swirl punch; chalk

2 Little Hands

Michelle captures the wonder in her daughter the day she discovered her hands. Mat photo on yellow cardstock. Journal on pink vellum; add chalk and pen details. Assemble border with squares cut from patterned and textured cardstocks. Embellish with patterned vellum, torn mulberry paper, brads, embroidery floss, buttons, punched shape, paper clip, wire and beads.

Michelle Loffler, Ferntree, Victoria, Australia

MOST POPULAR BABY NAMES IN 1902

BOYS	GIRLS
John	Mary
William	Helen
James	Anna
George	Margaret
Joseph	Ruth
Charles	Elizabeth
Robert	Marie
Frank	Lillian
Edward	Florence
Walter	Alice (and) Rose

Supplies: Patterned paper/(source unknown); die-cut letters/QuicKutz; word definitions/Making Memories; pink cardstock; gold embossing powder

A Newborn, A New Day

Tina captures the promise of a new day and a new life with serene photos and subtle journaling integrated into the patterned paper design. Layer matted definition over photos matted with solid and patterned papers. Mount sliced border strips on pink cardstock background. Die cut title letters; emboss with gold powder. Outline leaves on patterned paper; integrate journaling among patterned paper design lines.

Tina Coombes, Langley, Berkshire, England

Forever Mine

A collaged page speaks ever so softly about the best Valentine's Day present Summer ever received. Crumple and flatten ivory cardstock; sweep green ink pad over front and back of textured cardstock. Cut pink mulberry and patterned paper into large triangles; tear one edge, layer and mount at upper right and lower left corners of page. Cut mesh into triangles; mount at each corner and stitch an "x" with embroidery floss. Draw photo frame outline on textured ivory cardstock. Punch through paper at center and tear along drawn line. Curl edges of torn paper. Tear small strips of pink mulberry paper; mount around outside of torn frame under rolled paper. Stitch rolled edges with embroidery floss. Tie fibers and embroidery floss on metal heart. Mount metal letters and heart on green cardstock; crop. Link letter squares together with embroidery floss. Stamp journaling and toile design on ivory cardstock; collage torn strips of patterned paper and pieces of mesh on journaling block. Cut into eight-sided shape; mat on green cardstock and attach eyelets. Tie fibers to metal flowers before looping through eyelets. Stitch "x" at four corners with embroidery floss. Apply adhesive around the outside edges of journaling block, leaving room for pull-out journaling block to slide in and out. Secure hidden journaling block with swirl clip.

Summer Ford, San Antonio, Texas

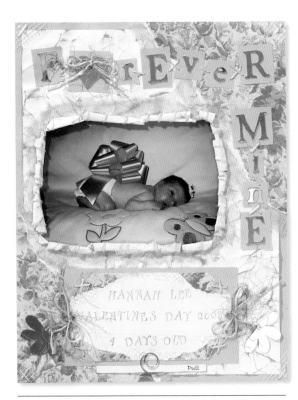

Supplies: Patterned paper/Anna Griffin; metal letters, metal heart, flowers, swirl clip/Making Memories; letter stamps/Hero Arts; toile stamp/Stampabilities; mesh/Magic Mesh; ivory and green cardstocks; pink mulberry paper; pink eyelets; green and pink fibers; pink embroidery floss; green ink

Comfort

Ronnie uses words to express how the desire for comfort is inherent in human beings. Print title and text on colored cardstocks. Layer red and green cardstock strips with enlarged photo over light green cardstock background. Vertically mount cropped duplicate photos over dark green strip. Mount text with green brads.

Ronnie McCray, St. James, Missouri

Supplies: Light green, green and red cardstocks; green brads

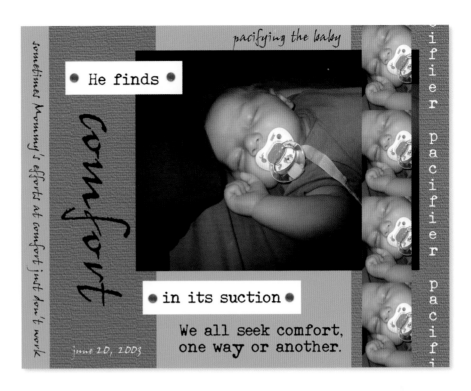

• He finds •

comfort

pacifying the baby

sometimes Mummy's efforts at comfort just don't work

june 20, 2003

• in its suction •

We all seek comfort, one way or another.

Hannah Noel

born 19 November, 2003
to Jake and Alicia Kuckartz
6 Pounds, 11 Ounces
19.75 Inches

Thy little life lies but within the compass of a dream,

and yet how changed does every scene of my existence seem

Emma Embury

Supplies: Black, white and burgundy cardstocks

MOST POPULAR BABY NAMES IN 2002

BOYS	GIRLS
Jacob	Emily
Michael	Madison
Joshua	Hannah
Matthew	Emma
Ethan	Alexis
Joseph	Ashley
Andrew	Abigail
Christopher	Sarah
Daniel	Samantha
Nicholas	Olivia

Hannah Noel

Suzanne shines a spotlight on a dream come true. Remove the background of the image and enhance the photo with photo-editing software, or re-create the same look by silhouette cutting the featured image from an enlarged photo. Journal on black background cardstock. Print title and large words from white and burgundy cardstocks; silhouette cut and layer on page.

Suzanne C. Walker, West Lafayette, Indiana

It is the morning of your life
and all your dreams are just beginning.

May you touch fireflies and stars,
dance with fairies, and talk to the man in the moon.

May you grow up with love and gracious hearts
and people who care.

Molly Grace Walker

Welcome to the world, little one.

It's been waiting for you

April Hardiwick

02.25.02

Molly Grace Walker

Suzanne wishes her newborn daughter a lifetime of love and a world of endless possibilities. Re-create sheer dimensional layers with a printed title and journaling on vellum. Horizontally layer monochromatic cardstock strips for background. Layer vellum across top and bottom of matted photo.

Suzanne C. Walker, West Lafayette, Indiana
Poem: April Hardiwick

Supplies: Vellum; shades of burgundy cardstocks

Cherish

Ralonda features a first-day photo that puts her tiny baby in perspective. Journal at bottom of red cardstock. Layer black cardstock and white patterned paper on red cardstock background. Mount torn patterned paper corner. Rub on white word transfer for title. Wrap ribbon across page; secure. Adhere sticker letters on red typewriter keys; mount on ribbon. Mat photo on lightly inked corrugated cardstock. Secure metal frame over cropped photo. Embellish corrugated die-cut hand with red ribbon, patterned paper strip, letter beads and heart nailhead.

Ralonda Heston, Murfreesboro, Tennessee

Supplies: Patterned papers/7 Gypsies/Hot Off The Press; letter stickers/Creative Imaginations; letter beads/Westrim; rub-on words, metal frame/Making Memories; die-cut hand/ American Tag Co.; heart nailhead/Scrapworks; typewriter keys/Magic Scraps; red cardstock; corrugated cardstock; gingham ribbon

Cherish

LOVE

You don't remember...
but I'll never forget

July 2 0 in 2001

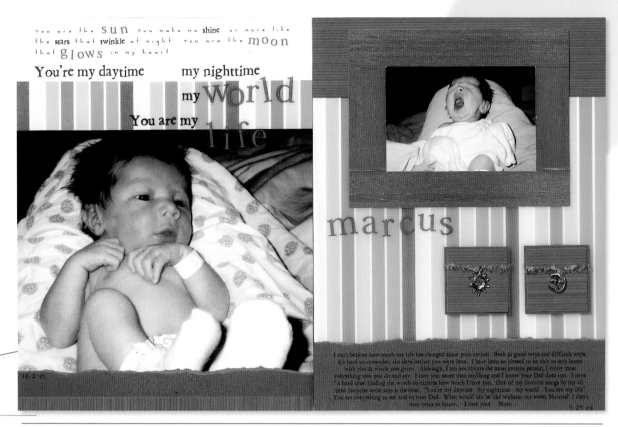

You are the **sun** You make me shine or more like
the **stars** that **twinkle** at night You are the **moon**
that **glows** in my heart

You're my daytime **my nighttime**

my WORLD

You are my

life

marcus

I can't believe how much my life has changed since your arrival. Both in good ways and difficult ways.
It's hard to remember the days before you were here. I have been so blessed to be able to stay home
with you & watch you grow. Although, I am not always the most patient person, I enjoy most
everything that you do and say. I love you more than anything and I know your Dad does too. I have
a hard time finding the words to express how much I love you. One of my favorite songs by my all-
time favorite artist says it the best. "You're my daytime my nighttime my world You are my life"
You are everything to me and to your Dad. What would life be like without our sweet Marcus? I don't
ever want to know. I love you! Mom   4-29-03

Supplies: Patterned papers/Paper Patch; patterned vellum, letter stickers/SEI; preprinted frame/My Mind's Eye; sun/moon charms/(source unknown); ivory, red and green cardstocks; fibers

You're My Daytime

Emily used lyrics to describe how the birth of her son has affected her life. Mount enlarged photo over patterned vellum strip on ivory cardstock. Layer torn red and sliced green strips at bottom of page. Print, stamp and adhere letter stickers for lyrics. Layer preprinted frame over photo; mount on green cardstock strip and patterned vellum layered over ivory cardstock. Journal on red cardstock; tear edge. Embellish green matted cardstock squares with charms hung from fibers.

Emily Garza, Layton, Utah

Sweet Dreams

Sweet Dreams

Tina used a color wheel to help her select tranquil yet contrast-ing colors for this peaceful page. Double mat photo on solid and speckled cardstocks; mount on patterned paper background. Adhere letter and metal stickers for title above layered cardstock strip. Mount metal handprint plaque.

Tina Coombes, Langley, Berkshire, England

Supplies: Patterned papers/(EK Success); letter stickers/(source unknown); metal letter tiles, metal handprint plaque/Making Memories; solid cardstocks

Every Good and Perfect Gift...

Terri snuggles photos of her son sleeping like an angel among soft, white textures. Mat photos on white cardstock; layer over ribbon mounted across torn mulberry paper. Journal on vellum; tear bottom edge.

Terri Davenport, Toledo, Ohio

Supplies: Mulberry paper/Printworks; white cardstock; vellum; ribbon

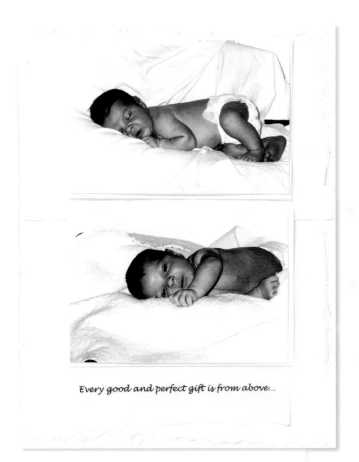

Every good and perfect gift is from above...

THE BEST GIFT MY CHILD RECEIVED

My husband started a tradition with the birth of our first baby. He gifted her with the singles (CD) of the #1 music hit on the day of her birth. In a couple of days she turns one and we're waiting to see just what #1 will be given to her this year. By her twenty-first birthday she will have all her music to laugh over, be embarrassed over or simply dance to.

Michelle Thompson, Somersham, Cambridgeshire, United Kingdom

My child received a baby nightgown with her name, her birth date and her weight embroidered across the front of it, also with a small Peter Rabbit on it. I was able to use it as an announcement for her arrival, and let people see her as well.

Mary Zimmer, New Baltimore, Michigan

Hospital Happenings

Nancy designed a simple layout that she can copy, modify and update while maintaining a consistent look throughout her son's baby book. Layer photos matted on green cardstock at right side of journaled ivory cardstock; mount on embossed cardstock background.

Nancy Korf, Portland, Oregon

Supplies: Embossed cardstock/Club Scrap; green and ivory cardstocks

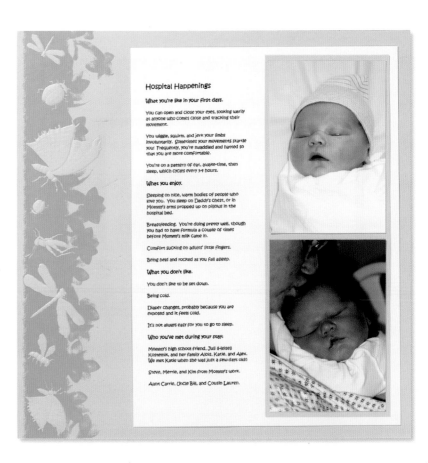

harrison robert foss

Every child born into the world is a new thought ...,
an ever-fresh and radiant possibility.

Kate Douglas Wiggin

what a surprise we had in you! our sweet baby boy could not
wait another 5 weeks to come into the world and made his
entry early. such a tiny little man, just 5 lbs 3 oz and 16.5
inches long. so very tired, we needed to wake you up to feed
you. so very beautiful. here on your second day of life.
welcome, welcome dear little one!

Supplies: Patterned paper/Lasting Impressions; safety pin nailheads/Jest Charming; yellow cardstock; fibers; eyelets

Harrison Robert Foss

Renee creates embracing warmth for her son's photos with soft shades of yellow. Tear yellow cardstock; mount over lighter toned yellow cardstock. Single and double mat photos on yellow and blue patterned cardstocks. Wrap fibers around extended second mat of one photo; attach safety pin nailhead. Print title, quote and journaling on cardstock in shades of yellow; mat. Attach eyelets; string or tie with fibers. Add pen detail around quote. Wrap left page with fibers; attach safety pin nailhead.

Renee Foss, Seven Fields, Pennsylvania

Treasured Gift

Torn paper and tied ribbons herald the arrival of Michelle's precious gift. Tear windows in blue cardstock background; mount large piece of yellow cardstock behind window at top of page. Tear window in yellow cardstock; chalk edges before rolling. Print title and text on a second piece of yellow cardstock; mount behind windows, positioning text in windows. Tie ribbon into bows; secure with wire and drape ends through small holes punched at corners and near title. Mount ribbon across bottom of page; push small "u" shaped wire over gathered section of ribbon through cardstock and twist to secure at back. Draw bear body parts on yellow and brown cardstocks; tear out. Detail with punched heart; chalk and pen. Layer bears over bottom corners of matted photo and ribbon. Assemble "gifts" from cardstock, ribbon and wire.

Michelle Murphy, Carver, Massachusetts

Supplies: Blue, brown and yellow cardstocks; gold ribbon; chalk; pen; wire

Hold On Little One

Keri offered comfort to her tiny newborn daughter by holding her hand. Layer patterned paper and red ribbon over burgundy cardstock background; slice window at bottom of page. Mount photo matted on black cardstock behind sliced window with foam spacers. Attach brad on patterned paper strip. Layer photo on black cardstock and yellow strip brushed with black ink; attach brad. Wrap metal heart with red fibers; secure around brad attached to black cardstock. Journal on yellow cardstock; tear and chalk edges before layering on patterned paper strip. Journal and attach metal phrase eyelet for title.

Keri Key, Burlington, North Carolina

Supplies: Patterned papers/Hot Off The Press/Wordsworth; metal phrase eyelet/Making Memories; burgundy, yellow and black cardstocks; fibers; brads; ribbon; chalk; black ink

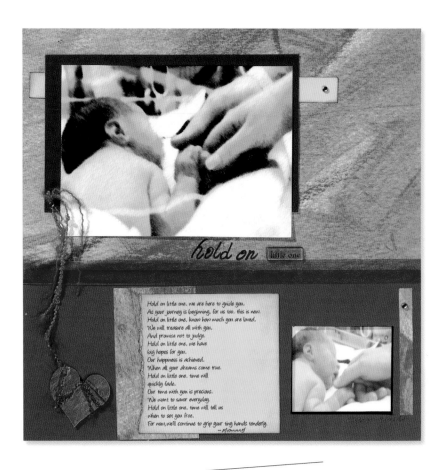

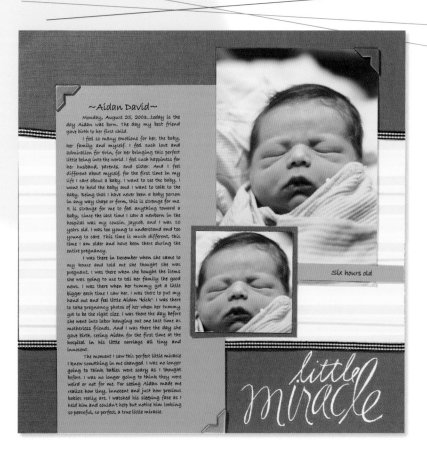

Little Miracle

Angela's journaling recounts the ways in which the birth of a close friend's baby touched her heart. Adhere ribbon along top and bottom edges of patterned paper mounted on green cardstock. Journal on green cardstock; layer with enlarged and matted photos and green cardstock strip. Mount photo corners. Rub on word transfer for title.

Angela Marvel, Puyallup, Washington

Supplies: Patterned paper/KI Memories; rub-on word, silver photo corners/Making Memories; green cardstock; ribbon

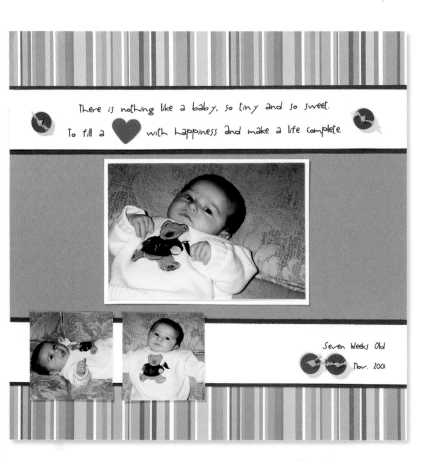

There is nothing like a baby, so tiny and so sweet. To fill a ♥ with happiness and make a life complete.

Seven Weeks Old
Nov. 2001

There Is Nothing Like a Baby

A striped border becomes this baby page. Slice two narrow strips of patterned paper and two narrow strips of navy cardstock. Horizontally mount patterned paper strips at top and bottom of green cardstock background. Print journaling on white cardstock; slice into strips that are slightly narrower than the previously cut navy strips. Mat white strips on navy strips and mount on page. Punch heart from red cardstock; mount among journaling. Tie buttons with fibers; mount on white matted strips. Mat large photo on white cardstock; crop smaller photos and mount.

Jennifer Bourgeault, Macomb Township, Michigan
Poem: Author unknown

Supplies: Patterned paper/Chatterbox; navy, green, red and white cardstocks; buttons; tan fibers; heart punch

THE BEST GIFT MY CHILD RECEIVED

My little brother, who was ten years old at the time, sewed my newborn, Matthew, a puppy. He cut the dog shape from dog printed fabric and stuffed it. I was in awe that he had done all this—I had never known him to sew, and while the stitches weren't perfect, the stuffed puppy was adorable. I now have it tucked away in Matthew's keepsake box.

Brandie Valenzuela, Victorville, California

Instead of giving us baby items when our second child was born, my mother gave us three house cleanings. It was a lifesaver!

Michelle St.Clair, Fuquay Varina, North Carolina

Dreams May Be Tough...

Ronnie sees her son as a tiny warrior raising his fist to fight off bad dreams. Re-create this computer-generated page by layering enlarged photo on solid and patterned papers on patterned cardstock background. Journal on green cardstock; attach with small brads. Mount partially cut or punched circles on opposite corners; stamp date. Assemble letter stickers and handcut letters for title.

Ronnie McCray, St. James, Missouri

Supplies: Patterned paper; solid paper; patterned cardstock; brads; circle punch; date stamp; letter stickers

july 5

Dreams may be Tough but I'm Tougher

James had his fist raised in his sleep, as if to ward off bad dreams. We know that it will be too soon that he won't need our comfort through bad dreams, but we hope he will always need our love.

These Precious Moments

Anne conveys warmth with a sepia-toned photo and mono-chromatic papers. Tear edges of patterned papers; layer and mount on ivory background cardstock. Print title and journaling on vellum; tear and chalk edges. Mount with eyelets. Camouflage hospital equipment with a self-adhesive vellum torn photo corner. Mat photo on peach cardstock; tear edges. Add flower stickers.

Anne Louise Rigsby, Cottonwood, Arizona

Supplies: Patterned paper/Paper Adventures; self-adhesive vellum/Emagination Crafts; flower stickers/Gifted Line; ivory and peach cardstocks; eyelets; brown chalk

An Angel Named Nanny

Christine honors her son's guardian angel on this beautiful mono-chromatic page. Print partial title and journaling on tan cardstock; tear two edges and mount on textured and stitched background paper. Double mat photo on tan cardstock and torn mulberry paper. Adhere letter stickers to cardstock; cut to size and mount on page with foam spacers. Mount pre-made tag and adhere flower stickers.

Christine Drumheller, Zeeland, Michigan

Supplies: Textured stitched paper/Provo Craft; letter stickers, flower stickers/K & Co.; tag/EK Success; tan cardstock; mulberry paper

June 2, 2002

Blessing Day

In Your Blessing, Your Father Blessed You With
Health & Strength
Kindness & Compassion for Others
The Desire To Follow Our Heavenly Father
The Desire to Follow the Prophet
To Someday be Married in the Temple
and Raise a Righteous Family
To Develop Your Talents & Gifts
To Learn Things Both Temporal & Spiritual
To Know That Your Family Loves You
To Be An Example To Those Around You

Supplies: Vellum; off-white cardstock

Blessing Day

Amanda displays a meaningful blessing given to her daughter with a symbolic overlay. Re-create the look of text superimposed on a photo by printing title and journaling on vellum sheets. Cut window to frame photo in large journaled vellum sheet; layer over photo mounted on cardstock background. Layer journaled vellum over enlarged photo on right page.

Amanda Behrmann, Austin, Texas

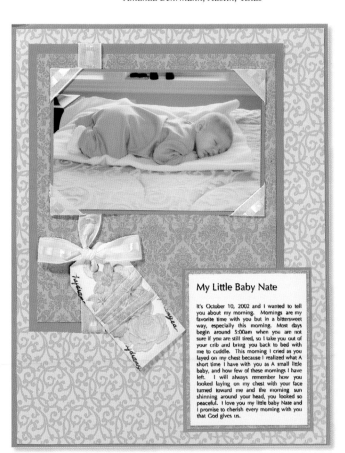

My Little Baby Nate

It's October 10, 2002 and I wanted to tell you about my morning. Mornings are my favorite time with you but in a bittersweet way, especially this morning. Most days begin around 5:00am when you are not sure if you are still tired, so I take you out of your crib and bring you back to bed with me to cuddle. This morning I cried as you layed on my chest because I realized what A short time I have with you as A small baby, and how few of these mornings I have left. I will always remember how you looked laying on my chest with your face turned toward me and the morning sun shinning around your head, you looked so peaceful. I love you my little baby Nate and I promise to cherish every morning with you that God gives us.

My Little Baby Nate

Christine documents a memorable journal entry on a stunning page. Mat patterned background paper and photo on green cardstock. Wrap corners of photo with ribbon. Stamp flower name on tag; chalk edges before layering embossed flower stickers. Wrap sheer ribbon around tag two times; secure ends. Cut a large square of coordinating patterned paper; mat on green cardstock. Wrap ribbon around matted patterned paper; attach tag and tie bow. Print journaling on cardstock; crop and double mat.

Christine Drumheller, Zeeland, Michigan

Supplies: Patterned paper/Making Memories; flower stickers/K & Co.; word stamp/ Stampa Rosa; green and ivory cardstocks; tag; satin and sheer ribbons; brown chalk

Sweet Baby Connor

Jennifer layers pastel cardstocks and tiny buttons for a snugly layout. Print journaling on pink cardstock; cut to 8½" high and mount near top of white cardstock background. Double mat enlarged photo on white and green cardstocks; mount at right edge of pink cardstock. Stamp journaling under photo. Slice strips of coordinating cardstock in a variety of widths; horizontally mount on page. Print large title letters onto colored cardstocks; silhouette cut and lightly ink edges of letters and mount on wide yellow strip. Stamp small title letters. Layer extra thin cardstock strips on wide strips; mount colored buttons. Stitch pacifier charm to page with embroidery floss.

Jennifer Bourgeault, Macomb Township, Michigan

Supplies: Letter stamps/PSX Design; charm/(source unknown); buttons; pink, yellow, white, and green cardstocks; blue and black inks; yellow embroidery floss; pastel buttons

Love You Forever

Tina sends her baby love with large dangling embossed letters. Cut large pieces of patterned paper; lightly ink edges and layer on white cardstock background. Mount silver embossed photo corners on bottom corners of enlarged photo. Print journaling and initial on tag; lightly ink edges and tie with ribbon. Print title letters on white cardstock; cut into rectangles and ink edges before mounting under photo. Print large "XO" letters on patterned paper; silhouette cut. Press letters onto embossing pad; sprinkle with extra thick embossing powder and heat. Repeat. Attach four eyelets at top of page; string elastic cord through eyelets and secure on back of page. Punch a tiny hole at the top of each embossed letter; attach safety pin and dangle from elastic cord. Secure dangling letters to page.

Tina Barriscale, Saskatoon, Saskatchewan, Canada

Supplies: Patterned papers/Anna Griffin/7 Gypsies; silver embossed photo corners/Magenta; white cardstock; tag; black ribbon; elastic cord; safety pin; extra thick embossing powder; black ink; eyelets

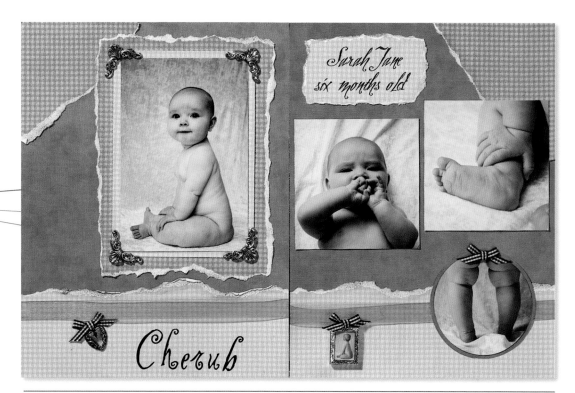

Supplies: Patterned paper/Daisy D's; letter stickers/Creative Imaginations; decorative corners/With Charm; heart charm/(source unknown); green cardstock; sheer and gingham ribbons; chalk

Cherub

Decorative silver elements lend a classic quality to cherubic photos of Andrea's daughter. Tear and chalk corners of green patterned paper; mount on green paper background. Double mat photo on pink and green patterned papers; tear and chalk edges of second mat. Mount decorative corners. Layer sheer green ribbon over pink patterned paper under torn and chalked edge. Adhere title letter stickers. Journal on pink patterned paper; tear and chalk edges. Tie ribbon to heart and small frame charm mounted with photo. Mat circle-cut photo on green cardstock and attach bow.

Andrea Hautala, Olympia, Washington

Bathing Beauty

Candi offsets her daughter's photos with vibrant colors and ruffled ribbon. Slice two narrow strips of patterned paper; mount above and below cropped photos on coral cardstock background. Mount ruffled ribbon on patterned paper strip below photos. Stamp title word; adhere sticker letters. Print journaling on transparency; mat on patterned paper.

Candi Gershon, Fishers, Indiana

Supplies: Patterned paper/Chatterbox/Cut- It -Up; sticker letters/Creative Imaginations; letter stamps/PSX Design; coral cardstock; black ink; ruffled ribbon; transparency

As a baby, your cries were virtually constant. Knowing we had met all of your needs to the best of our abilities, we simply couldn't understand your sadness. Realizing now what an active, driven child you are, I'm guessing that you felt like a quadriplegic trapped inside a body that wouldn't cooperate with your desires. You must have been totally miserable! Although you met all of the developmental milestones early, it simply wasn't quickly enough to satisfy your wishes. This is a photo of you taken at five weeks of age. At this point you were already rolling over regularly, however, I can see in your eyes the look of an energetic, determined child trapped inside a baby's body.

TRAPPED

in a baby's body

Move in for a CLOSE-UP

Every parent knows that the heart of a child does not reside in its tiny chest—it beats somewhere behind those baby blues. That's where tears and mischievous twinkles lie nestled behind fluttering lashes or slumbering eyelids. In search of clues that tell us more about our baby, we spend countless hours peering into tiny pairs of eyes. There we find intelligence, humor, fear, determination and, most of all, trust. Trust that we will love and care for our child until the world reverses its rotation. Close-up photos of your baby are as intimate as a kiss. In those pictures you can see more than just a face—you find glimpses of who he is and will become. Preserve special close-up photos of your child on pages that showcase dewy skin, angel-feather hair and eyes that offer an inroad to your baby's soul.

The face of Garbo is an Idea, that of Hepburn, an Event.
Ethel Barrymore

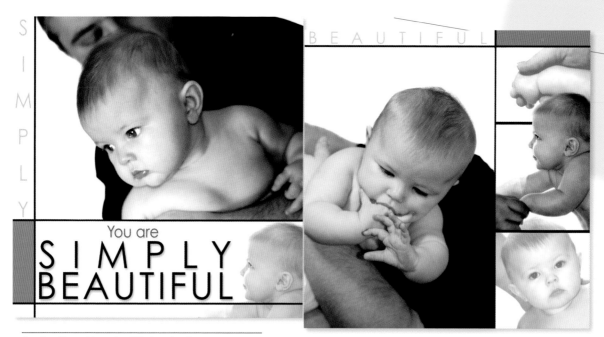

Supplies; Gray, white, red and black cardstocks; transparency

You Are Simply Beautiful

Clean lines, layered silhouette images and a bold splash of color give Denise's layout the look of a professionally designed advertisement. Enhance and enlarge photos with photo-editing software or with photo enlargements reproduced in shades of gray; silhouette cut. Vertically and horizontally layer thin black strips under and over photos and red cardstock on white cardstock background as shown. Print title and descriptive words on transparency.

Denise Docherty, Falkirk, Scotland

Bright Smile, Blue Eyes

Bluer than blue, baby's eyes stand out with a monochromatic background and inked metal embellishments. Divide page into quadrants; cut blue cardstock to fit quadrants. Press blue ink pad on star eyelets, metal mesh and swirl clips. Sprinkle with clear extra thick embossing powder and set. Enhance further by dabbing with diamond glaze. Wrap page with fibers and strings of silver beads. Layer photo on metal mesh before matting with blue metallic cardstock. Attach star eyelets at photo corners. Print title on white cardstock; silhouette cut. Print journaling on white cardstock; mat large journaling block on blue cardstock. Tuck corners into fibers and under mesh. Cut small journaling strip; mount beads at each end. Attach star eyelets at center of swirl clips.

Michelle Pendleton, Colorado Springs, Colorado

Supplies: Blue metallic cardstock/(source unknown); star eyelets/Stamp Doctor; diamond glaze/ JudiKins; metal mesh; blue ink; clear extra thick embossing powder; white and blue cardstocks; swirl clips; silver beads; fibers

Supplies: Patterned paper/Hot Off The Press; letter stickers/Pioneer; silver flower snaps, punched metal squares, silver metal word/Making Memories; leaves/EK Success; flower trim, velvet leaf/GreenPear.com; black cardstock; sheer black fabric; metal-rimmed tags; black ribbon; silver brads; black embroidery floss; flower button; silver leafing pen; crystal lacquer; circle punch; fabric; silk flowers

Precious

Bold color choices and floral embellishments make this page beyond precious. For left page, cut an 8 x 12" piece of patterned paper; tear bottom edge and mount on black cardstock. Mat photo on black cardstock; attach eyelets at bottom; dangle metal-rimmed tags tied with ribbon. Tear a vellum strip; layer under torn edge of patterned paper. Write title on vellum and dates on tags. Mount silver word next to vellum. Slice 2¼" and 1" black cardstock strips and a 1½" strip of burgundy patterned paper. Wrap the wider black strip with sheer black fabric, adhering at back. Tear bottom of narrower black strip; layer on burgundy strip. Embellish with embroidered daisy on punched metal square and red silk flower layered over green velvet leaves. Attach flower snap at center of red silk flower. Mount small matted photo at bottom of border strip and daisy embroidery trim. Duplicate layered flower design from border strip and mount above silver word. For right page, tear a narrow strip of patterned rose paper; layer over a wider strip of burgundy patterned paper and mount on right. Mount three photos, tucking right edges under torn paper strip. Journal on vellum; crop and tear bottom edge. Mat on black cardstock strip wrapped with sheer black fabric. Assemble and mount silk, embroidered and button flowers with black and green velvet leaves together at bottom of journaling block. Place rose paper scrap under vellum with journaling. Dangle metal-rimmed tags from top of page with embroidery floss. Hang punched metal square with ribbon tied into a bow from small brad. Embellish metal square with daisy and patterned paper square. Mount daisy trim at right side of page; place punched metal square under one daisy. Re-create "typewriter keys" by layering black cardstock circles on silver buttons. Adhere letter stickers on punched circles; coat with crystal lacquer.

Michelle Pesce, Arvada, Colorado

Glasses

Carrie saw things in a whole new way when she discovered that her eight-week-old son needed glasses. Print title, date and journaling on ivory cardstock; mat photo with journaling on red cardstock. Layer over patterned paper matted on brown cardstock. Adhere small photos on charms; coat with clear lacquer. String charms on hemp and wrap around photo on tag.

Carrie O'Donnell, Newburyport, Massachusetts

Supplies: Patterned paper, tag/7 Gypsies; charms/www.absolutelyevery thing.com; ivory, brown and red cardstocks; clear lacquer; hemp

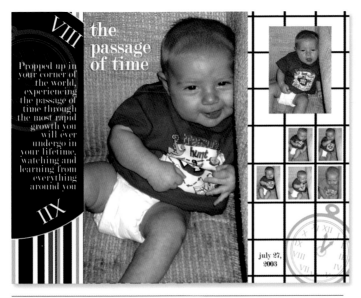

The Passage of Time

Ronnie symbolizes the brief period of her son's infancy compared to the rest of his life with a single color photo and monochromatic layout. Stamp clock on white and black cardstocks with gray or silver ink. Journal in reverse on stamped black cardstock; cut into large circle. Adhere letter stickers as Roman numerals; mount over striped patterned paper. Layer thin slices of black cardstock as a grid on background. Mount large and small photos; stamp date. Adhere white letter stickers for title.

Ronnie McCray, St. James, Missouri

Expressions in Blue

Dee utilizes a paint chip strip to express a range of emotional tones. Print title and photo captions on blue patterned paper; tear and chalk edges before mounting over blue cardstock background. Adhere letter stickers on small paint chip. Double mat large photo on blue cardstocks; mount next to paint chip strip. Punch photos into squares and mat; assemble across blue cardstock strip at bottom of page.

Dee Gallimore-Perry, Griswold, Connecticut

Bryce in the Bucket

An enlarged photo makes Amanda's son the focus of this joyful page. Slice a ½" and a 3½" strip of patterned paper and a ½" strip of blue paper. Horizontally mount narrowest strip of patterned paper near the bottom of tan cardstock background. Vertically mount the wider strip of patterned paper and the strip of blue paper on the left side of tan cardstock. Mount enlarged photo on page, keeping the corners free of adhesive. Circle crop one photo; layer with a larger tan circle cut to fit inside metal-rimmed tag. Fold corners of enlarged photo inward; secure with eyelets. Slip string from metal-rimmed tag under eyelet; attach. Mat remaining photo. Adhere title letter stickers; write remaining title words.

Amanda Goodwin, Munroe Falls, Ohio

Spiked

Denise makes a comical statement about her son's unmanageable hair through clever journaling. Mat patterned paper with black cardstock for background; wrap ribbon around top of page. String ribbon through metal buckle painted with ivory acrylic paint and tie. Mat all photos on black cardstock; mount on background with foam spacers. Print journaling on transparency, leaving room for metal eyelet letters. Paint metal letters with ivory acrylic paint before attaching to transparency. Print date on transparency; cut to fit inside metal-rimmed tag and tie with ribbon.

Denise Tucker, Versailles, Indiana

Supplies: Patterned paper/DMD; metal eyelet letters/Making Memories; black cardstock: transparency; metal-rimmed tag; gingham ribbon; metal buckle; ivory acrylic paint

Blue Eyes

Amy enhances her son's bright blue eyes with monochromatic layers of torn paper and textured elements. Tear strips of solid and patterned papers; layer on page. Mat photo on white cardstock. Stamp words on metal-rimmed tag and on torn strip. Twist paper wire into free-form shape; secure under brad on tag. Wrap mulberry spring roll across page; twist and secure under frame with eyelets.

Amy Warren, Tyler, Texas

Supplies: Patterned papers/Creative Imaginations/Lasting Impressions/ Provo Craft; mulberry spring roll/Pulsar; letter stamps/PSX Design; metal-rimmed tag and silver frame/Making Memories; white cardstock; brad; paper wire; eyelets

Supplies: Patterned vellum/Hot Off The Press; letter stamps/Stampin' Up!; white mulberry paper; pink textured and white cardstocks; white ink; pink ribbon; eyelets

Pretty in Pink

Summer showcases her daughter in eight different outfits on a softly feminine page. On the left page, mat four photos on one piece of white mulberry paper; tear edges. Silhouette cut flowers from patterned vellum paper; mount along bottom of page and photos. Stamp and emboss title on pink textured paper; slice into strip and mount at top of page. Layer a narrow strip of white cardstock over a torn strip of mulberry paper; mount under title and attach two eyelets at the center of the white strip. String pink ribbon through eyelets and tie into a bow. Print dates and journaling on white cardstock and vellum. Cut dates printed on cardstock into tags; mat on textured cardstock and attach eyelet at one end. Embellish with patterned vellum silhouette-cut flowers. Tie one tag to end of ribbon at top of left page. Heat emboss journaling printed on vellum. Attach at the center of textured cardstock background with eyelets; tie with ribbon. Mount three photos at top of right page over narrow strip of white cardstock layered over torn mulberry paper strip. Double mat remaining photo on white cardstock and torn mulberry paper; layer tag with ribbon over photo.

Summer Ford, San Antonio, Texas

Precious Little One

Jennifer touches upon the sweet essence of her son's infancy with sheer layers and delicate beaded details. Layer mesh strip, torn blue vellum and torn pink patterned strips over blue cardstock background. Stitch along torn vellum edge. Mat preprinted quote on blue cardstock and large photo on white cardstock. String beads on wire; curl ends. Mount with quote and letter stickers around photo. Wrap white slide mount with embroidery floss and beaded wire. Dangle charm with beads at center of slide and mount over blue cardstock. Rub word transfers onto photos.

Jennifer Brookover, San Antonio, Texas
Photos: Linda Luttbeg, San Antonio, Texas
Poem: Maureen Hawkins

Supplies: Patterned papers/Creative Imaginations/Lasting Impressions/Provo Craft; mulberry spring roll/Pulsar; letter stamps/PSX Design; metal-rimmed tag and silver frame/Making Memories; white cardstock; brad; paper wire; eyelets

The Eyes Are the Window to the Soul

Vicki surrounds a priceless photo with an embellished distressed frame. Layer patterned papers for background; mount satin decorative trim over paper seams. Stitch buttons. Cut apart preprinted frame; sand and ink edges. Reassemble over photo; attach brads. Dangle metal oval frame from bow. Adhere number sticker on ivory cardstock cut to fit inside oval frame; stamp word. Assemble title from letter stickers and printed letters. Attach hinge to inked ivory cardstock and page with small brads; adhere letter stickers. Journal on ivory cardstock; mount under hinged flap.

Vicki Harvey, Champlin, Minnesota

Supplies: Patterned papers/Daisy D's/Patchwork Paper; preprinted frame/Leeco; letter stickers/Creative Imaginations/Provo Craft; printed letters/Foofala; letter stamps/Hero Arts; number sticker/EK Success; ivory cardstock; satin decorative trim; sheer ribbon; brads; hinge; metal oval frame; buttons; ink

My Little Man

Joanne selected brown paper bag paper to symbolize her desire to package "don't forget" moments with her son. Slice section of patterned paper along printed design lines. Journal on ivory cardstock; tear bottom edge and slip under sliced section. Mat photo on ivory cardstock; layer over green and red cardstocks with torn edges. Pierce holes in green cardstock; stitch with jute string. Attach eyelets at center of preprinted stars; tie with jute string and dangle from stitched green cardstock. Embellish preprinted tag with eyelet and jute string.

Joanne Lee, Cape Elizabeth, Maine

Supplies: Patterned paper, preprinted embellishments/EK Success; date stamp/Making Memories; ivory, green and red cardstocks; eyelets; jute string

Discover

Vikki's folded edges add dimension and a fun flair to torn paper strips. Tear right edge of patterned paper and solid cardstock; layer with matted photo on tan cardstock background. Mount preprinted definition on brown and black cardstocks; tear and chalk edges. Attach eyelets. Journal on tan cardstock; integrate stamped letter tag and letter stickers with journaling. Wrap ribbon across page; mount frame over cropped photo.

Vikki Hall, Rogers, Arkansas

Supplies: Patterned paper/7 Gypsies; letter stickers/EK Success; definition sticker, metal frame/Making Memories; tan, black and brown cardstocks; gingham ribbon; small tag

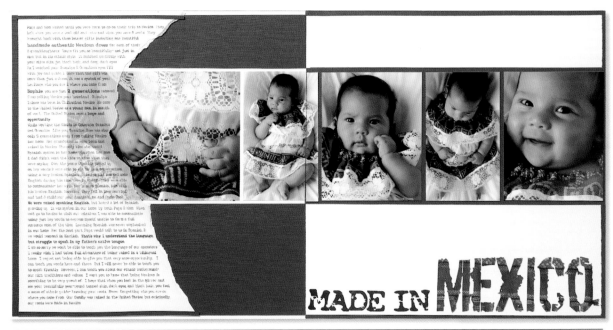

Supplies: Patterned vellum/Hot Off The Press; letter stickers/Creative Imaginations; purple and white cardstocks; vellum; fabric color copy

Made in Mexico

A handmade gift motivates Renee to journal the details of her family's heritage for her daughter. Mat purple cardstock on white cardstock for left page. Journal on vellum; mount over white cardstock and tear right edge. Mat two photos on white cardstock, leaving space between photos. Layer in between journaled vellum and white cardstock layers. Continue succession of photos on right page; mat on purple cardstock. Mount thin strips of purple cardstock around edges of white cardstock background. Color copy fabric of dress in photos; print title word in reverse on back of color copy. Silhouette cut letters and mount with black letter stickers along bottom of page.

Renee Villalobos-Campa, Winnebago, Illinois

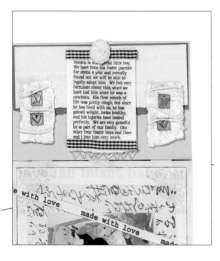

Supplies: Patterned papers, white metal plaque, printed twill/7 Gypsies; T-shirt transfer paper/Avery; letter template/Scrap Pagerz; letter beads/(source unknown); stickers/Creative Imaginations; stamps/Inkadinkado; silver charms/Card Connection; silver quote plaque/Making Memories; plastic heart/Handmade Creations; silver oval frame/Hirschberg, Schutz & Co.; fibers; ribbon; burlap; fabric; lace; microscope slide; mesh; slide frames; buttons; embossing powder; ink; paper clip; chalk

Holden

Ann dedicates her time to things that matter most, whether it's fostering a child or creating a meaningful layout. Create title flap that lifts to show hidden journaling with 10 x 5" cardstock "hinges" mounted between cardstock panels. Make sure at least 2" of cardstock strip extends beyond the bottom of panels. Adhere ends of strips behind white cardstock page; score and fold over top of page. Lightly ink top half of white cardstock flap; layer bottom half with torn patterned paper and ribbon. Stamp slide mounts with word designs; adhere preprinted vellum words. Cut title; stamp and emboss. Lift flap; mat patterned paper on dark blue cardstock and tear bottom edges. Journal on cream cardstock, ink with watermark ink and emboss with pearl ultra thick enamel. Embellish with ribbon, button and beads. Crumple, flatten and ink torn white cardstock; mount charms and wrap with fibers. Layer stamped transparency with photo over patterned paper with stamped corners and inked edges. Mat on white inked and embossed cardstock. Wrap printed twill. String charms on wire; attach to white metal plaque and wrap across page. For right page, mount torn black patterned paper strips on inked and embossed blue cardstock background. Stitch torn edges. Transfer photo onto burlap with inkjet T-shirt transfer paper. Mount fabric strips at top of fabric photo; stitch buttons. Tear window and edges of patterned paper; layer over blue cardstock. Roll torn edges. Mount transparency behind windows before adhering on foam core cut with same-sized window. Collage mesh, lace, fibers, swirl clip, metal plaque, letter beads, and stamped microscope slide wrapped with wire on dark blue cardstock. Mount behind foam core frame on page. Embellish frame with plastic heart, frame and wire.

Ann McElfresh, Tempe, Arizona

Sweet Bryce

Soft stripes and fuzzy fibers accompany Amanda's heartfelt letter. Print journaling on green paper; mount on left side of patterned paper background. Mat photos with lavender paper. Cut tag from lavender paper; mat with green paper. Draw faint lines on tag with purple, pink and blue gel pens. Distress tag. Punch hole at top of tag and tie with fibers. Stamp one title word on green paper scrap; frame with bookplate and attach to tag with brads. Complete with handwritten title word and heart brads.

Amanda Goodwin, Munroe Falls, Ohio

Supplies: Patterned paper/KI Memories; letter stamps/(source unknown); bookplate/www.twopeasina bucket.com; white heart brads/Accent Depot; green and lavender papers; fibers; purple brads; colored gel pens; brown ink

Great Close-Up Photos

If close-up is good, then super close-up can be even better. These up-close-and-personal spreads (pages 48-51) are sure to help you overcome any qualms you may have about capturing visual details and allow you to move in for those intimate photos.

Sweet Perfection

Closely cropped photos reveal tiny yet perfect features. Slice a narrow strip of black cardstock; mount at top of blue cardstock background. Mount a large piece of patterned paper on background. Print journaling on vellum; cut and mount at top of patterned paper. Double mat large photo on white and black cardstocks; stitch border with embroidery floss. Wrap top left corner of matted photo with ribbon; mount. Embellish around matted photo with shaped wire, letter tiles and a rattle sticker. String alphabet beads onto wire earring hoop; tie to ribbon at bottom of page. Rub on large title word transfer. Mat four cropped photos on one piece of black cardstock, leaving space between. Layer over ribbon vertically mounted on right side of page. Print date on ivory cardstock; trim to fit inside clear index tab. Slide tab under bottom photo. Add blue bow to top of matted photo strip.

Valerie Salmon, Carmel, Indiana

Supplies: Patterned paper/7 Gypsies; rub-on title word transfer/ Making Memories; letter tiles, alphabet beads, wire/Westrim; baby rattle sticker/EK Success; black, ivory and blue cardstocks; vellum; gingham and blue ribbons; wire earring hoop; white embroidery floss; clear index tab

Children Are Love

Peggy's use of graphic designs enhances the drama of black-and-white photos. Slice strips of patterned paper; sand paper edges. Mount preprinted tags on white cardstock squares; draw border and dot with black pen. Attach conchos over two tags and brad on another. Crop photos and layer with patterned paper strips on black background. Adhere quote sticker and journal on white cardstock; add penned border and dots. Layer over photo and patterned paper strip; attach square brads.

Peggy Roarty, Council Bluffs, Iowa

Supplies: Patterned paper, preprinted tags/KI Memories; quote sticker/Wordsworth; conchos/Scrapworks; black brads; white and black cardstocks; square brads; black pen

Supplies: Pearlized cardstock; pink and gray cardstocks; vellum; removable adhesive

And Baby Makes Three

Sliced windows invite the eye to look carefully at the elements which tell Evangelynn's story. Mat photos on gray and pink pearlized cardstock; mount on pink cardstock background. Print title on gray and pink cardstock; silhouette cut large title words. Cut small title words and mat on dark gray cardstocks. Lay vellum over page; draw squares around photo elements that will be viewed through sliced windows. Mount vellum over dark gray cardstock with removable adhesive; using a craft knife and straightedge ruler, cut through vellum and cardstock to create windows. Remove vellum; cut frame from pink pearlized cardstock and mount around center window. Journal on gray cardstock; mat on pink cardstock and mount on back of windowed page.

Evangelynn Lenz, Buckley, Washington

GETTING THAT PERFECT BABY PORTRAIT

Capture the best possible portrait of your baby by following these points:

- Plan your portrait session around your child's day. Do not take a tired child to a studio for a session. Early in the morning or soon after nap time are optimal times to schedule the picture.

- Feed your child before dressing her for the studio session. A hungry or thirsty child can be cranky.

- Select outfits that are not heavily patterned. Patterned fabrics tend to draw the eye away from the photo subject.

- Select an outfit in which your baby is comfortable. Hats are workable as long as your baby is cool wearing a hat.

- Bring along some of your baby's favorite toys as well as her blanket or love object.

- Do not attempt to coach your child before the photo shoot. "Practicing" smiles or poses results in photos that lack a natural spontaneous feeling.

- Discuss any concepts you have for the photo with the photographer prior to beginning the photo shoot. With small children it is often best for a parent to be in the studio during the photo session because your presence can provide emotional support and prevent separation anxiety.

- Offer to assist the photographer during your child's photo shoot but do not attempt to take over. The photographer has worked with many children in the past and has established his own methods for achieving that perfect expression.

- Don't give up immediately if your baby is whining or crying. Allow the photographer to spend some time with your child. Your baby may relax and cooperate if she has time to get to know and trust the photographer.

- If, after some time, it is obvious that your baby simply isn't in the mood for the photo session, take a break. Calm her down outside the studio and then try again. If the second attempt doesn't work, just call it a day and reschedule.

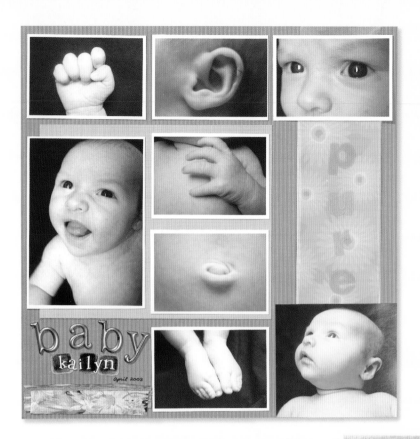

Baby Kailyn

Candi captures her newborn's tiny features with an array of closely cropped photos. Mat all but one photo on white cardstock. Layer three photos over light green patterned paper square before mounting on brown patterned paper background. Adhere green letter stickers to patterned vellum strip; mat on yellow patterned paper. Mount dimensional letters and letter stickers at lower left corner of page. Layer ribbon over paper yarn under letter stickers.

Candi Gershon, Fishers, Indiana

Supplies: Patterned papers/Chatterbox; patterned vellum/(source unknown); letter stickers, silver dimensional letters/Creative Imaginations/Mrs. Grossman's; white cardstock; ribbon; paper yarn

GET REALLY CLOSE

Think "close-up" and most often it's a face that fills the frame of your imagination. However, there are many wonderful opportunities for close-ups that will enrich your baby's scrapbook album. Consider taking up-close-and-personal pictures of your baby's:

• Feet	• Toes	• Hands
• Fingers	• Ears	• Mouth
• Eyelashes	• Eyes	• Belly
• Knees	• Ankles	• Dimples
•Toys	• Shoes	• Clothes
• Safety pins	• Rattles	• Bottles
• Tears	• Blanket	• Hair and hairbrush
• Toothbrush	• Tooth	• Spoons, cup and bowl

• Folds where thighs meet buttocks or the back of her neck

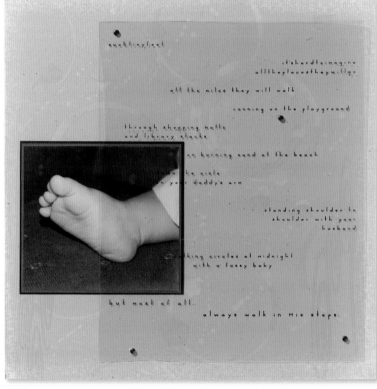

Supplies: Patterned cardstock/Club Scrap; maroon and black cardstocks; transparency; silver brads

Such Tiny Feet

Elizabeth imagines the miles her daughter's tiny feet will travel. Double mat photo on maroon and black cardstocks. Print text on transparency; partially layer over photo and patterned cardstock background. Attach small brads.

Elizabeth Ruuska, Rensselaer, Indiana

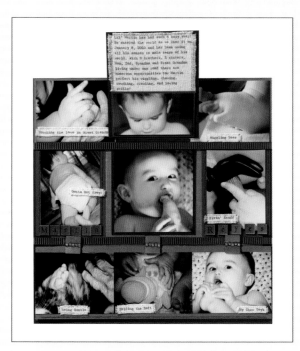

Supplies: Patterned paper/(source unknown); metal letter tiles/Making Memories; teal and blue cardstocks; blue ribbon; muslin fabric; hinges

So Very Busy

Andrea assembles an interactive layout with lift-up photo panels that accentuate the theme of a very busy baby. Divide page into three horizontal sections. Layer blue patterned paper, teal cardstock and blue ribbon in first section. Mount metal letter tiles, attach rivet. Mat single photos on cardstock; mount two photos on both sides of title. Mount three matted photos in middle section; stitch vertically along matted edge of photos at sides of page. Wrap ribbon across page above and below photos. Create a "hinged" photo flap over center photo. Cut a narrow cardstock strip the width of matted photo; horizontally score and fold in half. Adhere one panel of "hinge" between matted photo and background, and the other panel between layers of triple-matted photo. Create lift-up panel in third section from succession of three photos matted on one piece of blue cardstock; leave ¼" of matting above and below photos. Stitch along bottom of mat; mount one end of each hinge at top of mat. Mount photos on back of hinged panel; attach hinge to page over ribbon. Lift panel; mount photos matted on one piece of teal cardstock. Print photo captions and journaling on muslin fabric. Mount journaling inside center flap; layer captions on photos. Mount metal letter tiles for name.

Andrea Lyn Vetten-Marley, Aurora, Colorado

SET UP A GARAGE PHOTO STUDIO

More and more scrapbookers are setting up their very own photo studio in their garages. It saves scrapbook photographers from having to invest in expensive studio lights and the results are often amazing.

- Open your garage door wide.

- Set up an area for your garage studio that falls just outside the sweep of direct incoming sunlight. You do not want the sunlight to fall directly on your subject.

- Purchase a large piece of fabric or find an old bedsheet to use as a backdrop. Very dark or very light colors work best because they do not compete with the subject's skin tones. Do not fold or crease the material. Get rid of creases by throwing the material into your dryer.

- Use duct tape to secure the backdrop material to your garage wall. If a wall is not available, drape the material over a length of PVC extended between two ladders. If you are shooting a small child or a subject seated on the floor, you may drape the backdrop over the back of a chair or over a broom handle extended between two chairs.

- Drape the backdrop material so that it forms a gentle curve where it meets the floor. Extend it in all directions so that you can see no edges when looking through your viewfinder.

- Shoot pictures in your garage studio at different times of the day. You will find that your results vary depending on the angle of the sun.

- If you have no garage in which to set up your studio, consider using a large porch. The area must have some type of protective roof or overhang in order to diffuse direct overhead lighting.

IF I COULD SCRAPBOOK ABOUT JUST ONE OF MY CHILD'S TRAITS

I would capture my son's enthusiasm for discovery. It continues to amaze me how the simplest things are so interesting to him. He is fascinated with grass, flowers, twigs and even the inside of a refrigerator. Nothing excites him more than seeing a door or a baby gate left open.

Valerie Salmon, Carmel, Indiana

The one trait of Matthew's that I would scrapbook is his cowlick that is right in the front of his head. When he was a newborn and had very little hair, we could see how it would part the hair different ways. We would watch the area week after week as the hair become longer and the cowlick seemed to disappear. But, it is still there, doing its own thing. No amount of water, hair spray, or styling gel will cure it. Even still, his cowlick is a part of him that we love and that makes him unique.

Brandie Valenzuela, Victorville, California

Supplies: Black, white and blue cardstocks; vellum

Aidan

Joanne creates an impressively large, silhouette-cut monogram for her baby. Mount photos clustered with black cardstock strips. Print title and journaling on vellum; mount on same- sized white cardstock and mat on blue cardstock. Print letter "a" on blue cardstock; silhouette cut.

Joanne Lee, Cape Elizabeth, Maine

A Battle of Wills

Joanna creates a bit of pop-art fun to look like a familiar soup label. Slice a 3" strip of both light blue and brown cardstocks; mount blue and brown cardstocks at top and bottom of page edges. Print text on white paper; create white type by placing "reversed" text over a square filled with color in a drawing program. Cut printed text to fit between 3" strips; mount at center of page. Slice narrow strips of maroon and blue cardstock; vertically mount maroon strip at left edge of layout. Horizontally mount blue strip near top of page. Punch circle from tan cardstock; lightly ink edges; mount to look like soup label. Crop enlarged photo; mount on right side of page. Adhere title letter stickers at right side of page. Print "soup" directions on paper. Cut; mat on brown cardstock and mount at bottom of page.

Joanna Bolick, Black Mountain, North Carolina

Supplies: Letter stickers/Creative Imaginations; light blue, brown, maroon, blue and tan cardstocks; white paper; black ink; circle punch

Little Boy Blue

Joanna softens a spread with warm printed vellum accents. Print poem on blue cardstock. Slice a strip of patterned vellum; vertically mount at right edge of page. Slice a narrow strip of rust cardstock; mount along bottom of page and wrap with raffia strips. Mount a large section of patterned vellum on white cardstock; silhouette cut flower from vellum and mount at left edge of page. Mount buttons under photo.

Joanna Bolick, Black Mountain, North Carolina

Supplies: Patterned vellum/Creative Imaginations; blue, dark blue, rust and white cardstocks; buttons; raffia

Baby Blue Eyes

Kimberly learned that trying to photograph a baby on the move can result in interestingly framed shots! Journal on blue cardstock; tear bottom edge and layer with torn patterned paper strip on dark blue cardstock background. Knot fibers and mount across bottom of page. Mat photo on white cardstock.

Kimberly Lund, Wichita, Kansas

Supplies: Patterned paper/Carolee's Creations; white, light and dark blue cardstocks; fibers

Supplies: Patterned paper/Karen Foster Design/Magenta/Paper Adventures; metal letters, silver charms/Making Memories; date stamp; tags; ivory cardstock; square punch; fibers; buttons; white tags

A Boy and His Buggas

Mary-Catherine documents her son's vocabulary of invented words he uses to express his fascination with bugs. Slip small photo under sliced corners of patterned paper; mat on ivory cardstock. Assemble title sticker and metal letters on ivory strips; layer on torn patterned paper strip over dark patterned paper background. Layer remaining photos over green patterned paper. Wrap fibers across one photo; dangle charm from fibers. Journal on ivory cardstock; tear bottom edge and mount on patterned paper. Punch patterned paper squares; mat on ivory cardstock. Download insect clip art from the Internet and print on small white tags; layer with buttons.

Mary-Catherine Kropinski, Maple Ridge, British Columbia, Canada

Cutie Pa-tootie

Brandy demonstrates that less is more with this powerful layout. Double mat photo on navy blue and orange cardstocks; tear and chalk edges of second mat. Stitch one button near top of yellow cardstock background leaving long ends to attach to torn matting. Pierce two small holes at top of torn mat; string fiber through holes and knot. Adhere "hanging" matted photo on page. Slice two very narrow strips of orange cardstock and one narrow strip of navy blue cardstock; horizontally layer near bottom of page leaving space between each strip. Layer metal frame over cropped photo; mount over horizontal strips. Stitch buttons along bottom of page.

Brandy Logan, Hendersonville, North Carolina

Supplies: Silver frame/Making Memories; navy, yellow and orange cardstocks; blue buttons; fiber; chalk

Supplies: Embossed patterned cardstock, letter stickers, embossed stickers/K & Co.; gold spirals/7 Gypsies; green cardstock; green vellum; gold brads; bow; brown ink

Spring Babies

A charming yellow bow adorned the hair of a birthday girl before it became the inspiration for Vanessa's layout. Layer torn embossed patterned cardstock with inked edges over green cardstock background. Double mat photos on patterned and embossed cardstocks; tear and ink bottom edges. Assemble title letter stickers on embossed patterned cardstock; attach brads on letter tags. Mount keepsake bow with title. Journal on green vellum; mount with brads. Embellish photos and title with embossed stickers, gold spirals and brads.

Vanessa Spady, Virginia Beach, Virginia

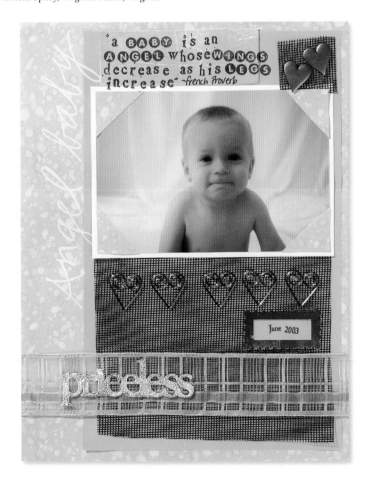

Priceless

Sam adds vibrant color and metallic shine to offset the stark white background behind her baby. Mat photo on white cardstock; mount photo corners cut from patterned paper. Layer with screen on green paper mounted on patterned paper background. Rub on white word transfer for title. Stamp quote on crumpled and flattened green paper strip. Attach heart eyelets on screen square; layer with photo mat. Adhere heart paper clips. Stamp date; mount behind frame. Wrap ribbon across page. Emboss metal word with white embossing powder; dab with ink and coat with clear extra thick embossing powder.

Sam Cousins, Shelton, Connecticut

Supplies: Patterned paper, white rub-on letters, metal word, date stamp, silver heart eyelets, silver frame, heart paper clips/Making Memories; letter stamps/Hero Arts/PSX Design; green paper; white cardstock; black screen; ribbon; clear extra thick embossing powder; white embossing powder; black ink

Supplies: Mesh/Magic Mesh; clock, text stamps/Rubber Stampede; brown, tan and pink cardstocks; wire; eyelet; chalk; metallic rub-ons

Time

Kristen contrasts a new life with the timeless look of aged accents. Print definition on brown cardstock; soak in water until ink begins to blur. Crumple and flatten; dry. Apply metallic rub-ons; tear and chalk edges. Layer over pink cardstock; tear and chalk edges and mat on tan cardstock. Print title on pink cardstock; silhouette cut and layer on stamped cardstock strip. Single and double mat photos on pink cardstock with torn and chalked edges and stamped cardstock. Journal on stamped cardstock; chalk edges and embellish with free-formed wire hearts and distressed cardstock scraps. Stamp text on tag; chalk edges and collage distressed cardstock, mesh, wire and silhouette-cut stamped clock. Apply metallic rub-ons over mesh. Attach eyelet over pink cardstock square; add curled wire.

Kristen Swain, Bear, Delaware

Sweater & Socks

A quaint vintage postcard inspired Candi to soften and distress patterned papers for a charming shabby chic layout. Diagonally layer torn patterned papers for background; curl torn edges. Attach rivets at opposite corners; sand small torn corner. Mat photo on lightly sanded patterned paper; layer over vintage postcard matted on patterned paper. Attach rivets on postcard mat; dangle metal-rimmed tag from fibers strung through rivets. Adhere letter stickers on colored tag; tear end and tie with ribbon. Sand bottom of patterned paper background; adhere letter stickers to complete title.

Candi Gershon, Fishers, Indiana

Supplies: Patterned paper/Chatterbox/KI Memories; letter stickers/Chatterbox/Doodlebug Design; tags/2 Dye 4; rivets; vintage postcard; fiber; ribbon; sandpaper

B Is for Baby

Elizabeth created an inviting layout for memorable first photos and thoughts. Print journaling on yellow textured cardstock background. Layer white handmade paper over green cardstock and yellow patterned paper. Mat photos and die-cut tags with green cardstock. Stamp title words on tags and patterned paper; mount tags on page with foam spacers. Adhere title letter pebbles. Enhance a pre-made tag; cut oval window at center. Mount piece of clear plastic cut larger than oval to back of tag; adhere over preprinted postcard with foam spacers. Adhere large sticker letter "B" at lower left corner of tag and mount.

Elizabeth Ruuska, Rensselaer, Indiana

Supplies: Yellow textured cardstock/Club Scrap; white handmade paper/(source unknown); patterned paper/KI Memories; letter sticker/Colorbök; letter stamps/PSX Design; letter pebbles/Creative Imaginations; pre-made tag/Me & My Big Ideas; preprinted postcard/Anna Griffin; green cardstock; black ink; tag die cuts; clear plastic sheet

Soft Touch

Gayle layers duplicate photos and patterned paper to accentuate a focal point. Diagonally tear ivory patterned paper; layer over blue patterned paper matted on beige cardstock. Layer tags with patterned paper, border stickers and stickers. Mat on ivory cardstock; chalk edges. Journal on vellum and tear edges; layer over large tag. Stamp postage stamp designs on smaller tags and attach eyelets. String fiber through eyelets and mount along border sticker; wrap fiber ends around brads. Print date on one of two 5 x 7" photos using photo-editing software. Crop one photo and mat on patterned paper; mount over second photo with foam tape. Adhere title letter stickers.

Gayle Hodgins, Philadelphia, Pennsylvania

Supplies: Patterned paper, letter stickers, border and coordinating stickers/Creative Imaginations; postage stamp/Inkadinkado; beige cardstock; vellum; eyelets; copper brads; fiber; chalk

Bobby

Wendy adds a modern twist to a vintage photo by altering images with photo editing software. Scan vintage photo, alter and print on photo paper. Slice photo into quadrants; tear outside edges and reassemble on patterned paper background, leaving space between sections. Die cut tag and letters from distressed paper. Stamp date on tag; attach feet brads and fibers. Layer negative space from die-cut letters over colored paper squares. Angle and mount die-cut letters over negative spaces. Wrap fibers across bottom of page; tie ends and secure under feet brads.

Wendy Bickford, Antelope, California

Supplies; Distressed paper/Rusty Pickle; die-cut letters, tag/Sizzix; date stamp/Making Memories; silver feet brads/www.Lifetimemoments.com; fibers

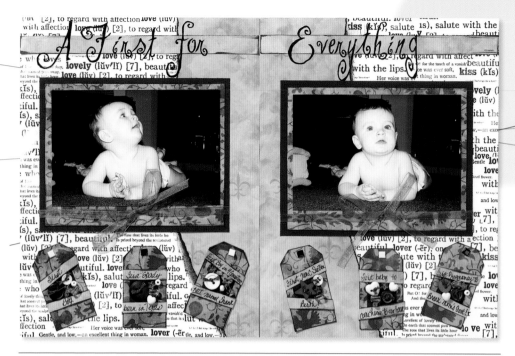

Supplies: Patterned paper/7 Gypsies/Creative Imaginations; letter stickers/Creative Imaginations; black cardstock; green paper; square brads; ribbon; green embroidery floss; beads; buttons; ink

A First for Everything

Vanessa proves that even a second child can be the source of many "firsts" with journaled and embellished tags. Tear and ink edges of green patterned paper; mount over white patterned background paper. Adhere title letter stickers over green patterned paper strips with inked edges. Double mat photos on patterned paper and black cardstock; tie ribbon around bottom of photos. Cut tags from patterned paper; ink edges. Slice narrow green paper strips; ink edges and wrap around tags before writing "firsts." Tie buttons with embroidery floss; mount with beads on tags. Attach to page with square brads.

Vanessa Spady, Virginia Beach, Virginia

IF I COULD SCRAPBOOK ABOUT UST ONE OF MY CHILD'S TRAITS

I would scrap about my baby's resolve to be his own person, despite developmental handbooks that defined what he should be doing and other people's assessment of what makes a "good" baby. If I could only scrap this one trait, it would still allow me to tell his story. From his 20-minute naps when I was hoping for two-hour ones, to walking at 8 months old, I never found the key to being his mom in a book. He has been his own person, against all my desires to make him the way I wanted him to be or the way others said he should be.

Ruthann Grabowski, Yorktown, Virginia

Mine!

Deborah admits that the apple doesn't fall far from the tree on a journaled tag detailing her daughter's determined temperament. Print title, photo caption and journaling on green and rust cardstocks; slice into strips and mount on patterned paper background. Mount matted photo over torn and chalked cardstock strips. Cut photo caption into tag; wrap with fiber and dangle word charm. Attach star eyelets.

Deborah Nolan, Indianapolis, Indiana

Supplies: Patterned paper/Paper Patch; word charm/Charming Pages; star eyelets/Making Memories; green and rust cardstocks; chalk; tag; fibers

Boy Oh Boy

Janice imports masculine copper and denim images into her computer-generated layout as faux dimensional embellishments. Re-create this page with embellishment images purchased from a digital scrapbook Web site. Journal on tan cardstock. Horizontally mount patterned paper. Stitch denim-colored cardstock strips; vertically mount as photo borders. Heat copper sheet over flame until color changes; bend slightly for dimension and cool. Attach eyelets and sun charm; secure on burlap fabric scrap with jump rings. Adhere black letter stickers on copper sheet; cut into shapes and mat on black cardstock.

Janice Dye-Szucs, Oshawa, Ontario, Canada

Supplies; Embellishment images/www.scrapbookgraphics.com; tan and blue cardstocks; copy sheet; eyelets; sun charm; burlap fabric; jump rings; letter stickers

BOY OH BOY

Do we ever have our hands full with you Mikaiah!! From the tip of your cute little nose to the twinkle of your sweet little toes, you are boy all boy through and through.

With dare-devil antics you throw yourself down the park slide backwards, head first and with no fear whatsoever!

Your a puddle jumper, a stone thrower and a stick collector. You think sand belongs in your hair and the other day you got down on all fours and licked up a bug!!

My heart skips a beat just to watch you in motion. Boy oh boy am I ever lucky that your mine.

Supplies: Patterned paper/Craft Print; textured metallic cardstock/(source unknown); preprinted tags/Hot Off The Press; green, cream and black cardstocks; embroidery floss; eyelets; chalk

Our Spring Flower

Michelle sowed a garden full of spring blossoms for her daughter, whose middle name, "Lani," is a New Zealand Maori word that means "flower." Layer solid cardstocks and patterned paper with torn edges over green cardstock background. Triple mat large photo on textured metallic and colored cardstocks; tear bottom edge of third mat. Print and silhouette cut title from black cardstock. Silhouette cut parts of flower from four sheets of same patterned paper; build layers over original image and mount with foam tape. Tear cream cardstock scraps; chalk and attach with eyelets. String embroidery floss through eyelets and tie to preprinted tags. Mat two photos on one piece of textured metallic cardstock.

Michelle Thompson, Somersham, Cambridgeshire, England

THREE

MASTER

of his

DOMAIN

The soft winds of the early summer whisper gently through the
Aspen trees in our back yard while Kyle has claimed the playhouse
as his domain for the season. The squeals and giggles of delight
can be heard when he is able to control who or what he lets into
"his" house. As the seasons change and so does my little blue-
eyed boy. With a tugging at my heart and a tear in my eye I
reflect upon his infancy and know each day he is growing up and the
playhouse is just the beginning of many things he will master.

KYLE PENDLETON
JUNE
2003
16 MONTHS

Lights, Camera, ACTION!

From mew to bellow to babbling "da-da's" and "ma-ma's" babies add their voices to the symphony of the human race. From swaying attempts to lift cumbersome heads, caterpillar belly ootches, to cantering crawls, babies physically become a part of the world around them. Their actions grow with their confidence and as such, timid bites of mushy cereal while belted securely in a high chair give way to voracious chomps on apple slices while toddling after the neighbor's dog or scaling a mini slide. If gentle photos of your newborn asleep tug at your heartstrings, photos of your baby in full-throttle motion—exploring the environment, exploding with opinion and demanding adoring attention—are some of the most dynamic you'll ever take. Scrapbook pictures of your baby in motion on pages that can stand up and scream, "Applause!"

> *Look, I don't want to wax philosophic, but I will say that if you're alive you've got to flap your arms and legs, you've got to jump around a lot, for life is the very opposite of death, and therefore you must at the very least think noisy and colorfully, or you're not alive.*
>
> **Mel Brooks**

All Boy

Susan makes colorful photos and creatively cut cardstock "romp" on this playful layout. Dampen and crumple tan cardstock; flatten and lightly ink creases. While damp, print title and stamp words; dry. Punch two holes at sides; mount washers over holes. String fiber through washers and tie; mount textured cardstock on yellow background cardstock. Cut red, yellow and blue cardstocks to continue the curves of playground equipment beyond the enlarged photo. Rub ink along the edges of red cardstock strips. Mount washers on cardstock mimicking placement in photo. Adhere letter stickers and stamp journaling on pre-made tags; attach safety pin and tie fiber to tags before layering on page.

Susan Cyrus, Broken Arrow, Oklahoma

Supplies: Letter stamps/Hero Arts; letter stickers/EK Success; pre-made tags/2DYE4; tan, yellow, red and blue cardstocks; black ink; tags; silver washers; fiber; safety pin

TAKE BETTER ACTION SHOTS

Whether your baby is in the squirmy, wiggly stage or a streak of motion, you'll want to capture his antics on film. Here are tips for capturing your tyke in-the-moment.

- Get down to your baby's level rather than shooting from above.

- If your child is old enough to "cheese" for the camera, photograph him with a zoom lens. This allows you to get close-up pictures without interfering with the natural play that is going on.

- Shoot action photos with faster speed film (400 or above).

- Set your shutter speed at $1/125$ or faster. This will allow you to take continuous photos, increasing the chances that you'll capture just the right moment.

Our Son Shine

Jennifer ties in the colors and designs on the her son's summer outfit in this happy summer spread. Crop photos; mat two on red and all on blue cardstock background. Cut title letters from blue and yellow cardstocks. Mat letters and silhouette cut; layer three on red cardstock scraps. Mount all letters on white cardstock; adhere red vellum flower sticker in place of "o" and stitch button at top of "i." Write title word and border. Tear yellow patterned paper to fit next to title; wrap with embroidery floss and stitch button. Layer clear plastic word tiles on colored cardstock rectangles with one torn edge; mat on white cardstock. Stitch buttons on yellow cardstock strip with embroidery floss; mat on white cardstock. Print journaling on white cardstock; cut into tag shape and tear bottom edge. Layer tag over torn yellow patterned paper and red cardstock. Draw border around tag. Stitch blue button on red rectangle folded over top of tag. Punch lattice design in white cardstock. Layer with yellow and red vellum flower stickers over alternating yellow and red cardstock rectangles.

Jennifer Brookover, San Antonio, Texas

Supplies: Patterned paper/(source unknown); lettering template/Scrap Pagerz; flower punch/Family Treasures; lattice punch/Fiskars; vellum flower stickers/EK Success; plastic word tiles/KI Memories; red, white, yellow and blue cardstocks; red, blue and yellow buttons; white embroidery floss

• Follow your baby's action through your viewfinder.

• Wedding photographers often focus the camera on one spot and wait for the action (the wedding party moving down the aisle, for example) to move into range before taking the photo. This practice can work when photographing babies as well. Set up your camera between your baby and an object he is sure to move toward (a cookie or a toy). Be prepared to snap the shutter as he moves into your camera's view. Be patient and wait until just the right moment.

• Take a lot of photos with the expectation that among the batch you'll find just the right picture, one that is in focus and captures an expression you'll cherish.

The Magic of the Sea

Marina remembers her daughter's first moments by the sea with a collection of treasures. Mount flattened ivory paper yarn over torn green and gray cardstock strips layered on blue cardstock background. String title glass and letter beads on wire; mount below twisted fibers and curled wire. Journal on vellum; tear and chalk edges. Wrap coastal netting across page; attach journaling with eyelets and embellish with glass pebbles, sand dollars, sea stars and gold shells.

Marina Dintino, Lansdale, Pennsylvania

Supplies: Letter beads/Westrim; netting; ivory paper yarn/Making Memories; green, blue and gray cardstocks; vellum; wire; eyelets; gold seashells; glass pebbles; sand dollars; sea stars; chalk

I'm On My Way...

Linda arranged words from a favorite song to tell the story of a little girl with an unstoppable spirit. Mount ribbon with inked edges across patterned paper; adhere title letter stickers and stamp words. Double mat photo on yellow and black cardstocks. Adhere poem stone, letter stickers and pebble; stamp date.

Linda Garrity, Kingston, Massachusetts
Photo: Cheryl Chapman, Kingston, Massachusetts

Supplies: Patterned paper/Karen Foster Design; letter stickers/Creative Imaginations/Me & My Big Ideas; letter stamps/PSX Design; date stamp/Making Memories; poem stone/ Creative Imaginations; yellow and black cardstocks; ribbon; black ink

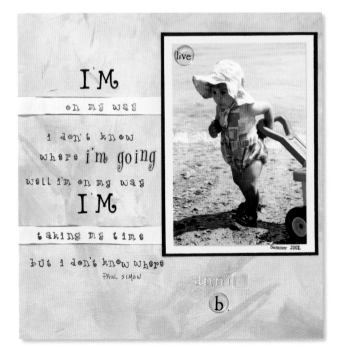

Supplies: Patterned vellum/Magic Scraps; letter stamps/ PSX Design; letter stickers/ Creative Imaginations; square brad/Making Memories; white cardstock; fibers

This End Up!

Sam selects a lively patterned vellum to emphasize her son's pleasure in the world down under. Mount patterned vellum on white cardstock with spray adhesive. Attach square brad; loop fibers around brad and over top of page. Wrap tied fibers across page and over photo. Adhere title letter stickers.

Sam Cousins, Shelton, Connecticut

One of Cade's favorite things to do is taking a bath. He loves it when his mommy pours water on him and he can sit in the tub and play with his toys. While we were visiting Mom and Mike, Linda had to use the deep sink in their laundry room to wash him since he still couldn't sit up on his own yet. But he didn't seem to care - as long as he could splash the water around and get clean - he was a happy baby!

Supplies: Patterned paper/Wubie; vellum phrases/Kopp Design; vellum; white and green cardstocks; silver brads

Squeaky Clean

Candice cleans up with a fresh layout that features her nephew's expressive face amongst thematic phrases. Mount succession of photos over blue patterned cardstock matted on white cardstock. Slice along duck's head and slip last photo behind sliced area. Journal and mount vellum title words on white cardstock; double mat and attach brads. Cut duck from printed vellum paper. Mount green cardstock corners on printed vellum phrases.

Candice Cruz, Somerville, Massachusetts

Water Everywhere

Jennifer's choice of cool preprinted designs contrasts photos of her boys splashing in the Texas heat. Single and double mat photos on solid and patterned papers. Cut apart preprinted designs, tags and photo corners. Single and double mat designs and tags. Mount watch crystal over blue beads. Stamp date.

Jennifer Stewart, Austin, Texas

Supplies: Letter beads/Westrim; netting; ivory paper yarn/Making Memories; green, blue and gray cardstocks; vellum; wire; eyelets; gold seashells; glass pebbles; sand dollars; sea stars; chalk

Explore

Valerie captures the rugged beauty of nature with torn and folded paper edges. Tear corner of patterned paper; mount at upper right corner of green cardstock background. Slice a narrow strip of blue cardstock; mount across bottom of page. Double and triple mat photos on patterned paper and light and dark blue cardstocks; tie fiber around bottom of one photo; mat. Tear edges of first photo mat; stitch border. Fold upper left corner of triple matted photo; secure with brad. Cut large tag from blue cardstock; stitch edges. Mount patterned paper strips on tag; stitch border and attach eyelet over blue cardstock square. Adhere letter stickers on title vellum tag; stitch on tag and tear edges. Print definition on green cardstock; layer over blue mesh scrap; stitch on tag. Embellish with fibers tied to tag and button. Print journaling on yellow vellum; layer over photos and border strip. Embellish with buttons and small tags attached with brads. Stamp letters on tags; stamp age and date on border strip. Layer label tape words and patterned paper strip on squares punched from blue paper. Mount on page.

Valerie Salmon, Carmel, Indiana

Supplies: Patterned paper/Creative Imaginations/Doodlebug Design; letter stickers/Creative Imaginations; mini tags/DMDs; green, light and dark blue cardstocks; vellum; yellow vellum; silver brads; fibers; buttons; label tape; large eyelet; blue and white inks; square punch

BABY TRIVIA

The heaviest baby at birth weighed 24 pounds.

The oldest mother on record was 63 years old.

The lightest baby at birth weighed 10 ounces.

The most surviving births from a multiple gestation is seven.

A baby chooses his mother's face over those of others as early as 2 weeks old.

An infant's head is one-fourth the size of the rest of his body.

Most babies begin smiling when 4-8 weeks old.

A baby can tell the difference between its mom's native language and other languages at birth.

All babies have blue eyes at birth but the color can change within moments of delivery.

Stacking Rings

A favorite slide from Elise's childhood is given new life and a burst of color with a scanner and photo-editing software. Cut colored cardstock into geometric shapes. Mount at bottom of black cardstock background. Slice a narrow strip of vellum; layer over geometric shapes and attach with eyelets. Triple mat photo with off-white cardstock and a multicolored paper.

Elise Desmarais, Montreal-Nord, Quebec, Canada
Photo: Claude Desmarais, Anjou, Quebec, Canada

Supplies: Black and colored cardstocks; computer-created patterned paper; colored eyelets; vellum

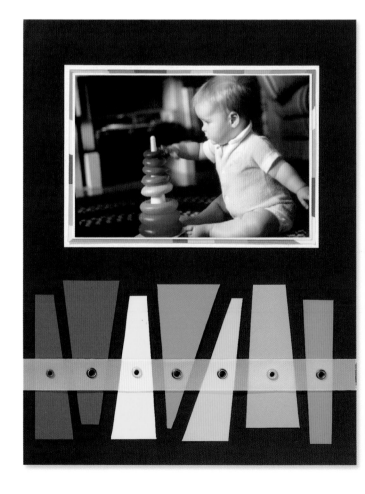

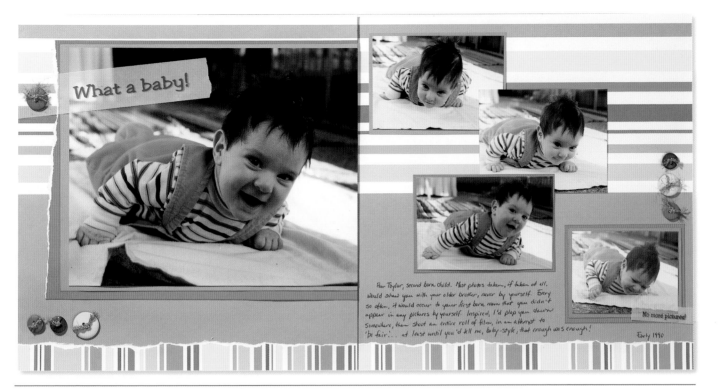

Supplies: Patterned paper/SEI; blue and red papers; vellum; fiber; buttons

What a Baby!

Gwyn mirrors her son's colorful personality with a bold striped border that matches the pattern on his shirt. Mount torn patterned paper strips at bottom of patterned cardstock background. Single and double mat photos on blue and red paper; tear second mat for enlarged photo. Print title and photo caption on vellum. Tie buttons with fibers.

Gwyn Calvetti, West Salem, Wisconsin

MY BABY TAUGHT ME

He had colic for five months; it was terrible, but it did teach me that no matter how tired and irritable I am, and how little sleep I've had, and how much he's screamed, when he goes to sleep, he is still so beautiful it is hard to resist the urge to pick him up and kiss him. Even in the worst of circumstances when a dark cloud seems to hang over every day, there is still an untapped wellspring of maternal love that nothing, absolutely nothing, can take away.

Shirley Bouwer, Eastbourne, East Sussex, United Kingdom

Discover

Amy catches a glimpse of an adventurous baby who loves to climb to new heights. Journal on patterned paper. Layer strips of patterned paper horizontally, vertically and diagonally around and over photo on red cardstock background. Attach square brads. Capture colored beads under watch crystal. Rub on word transfer for title. Adhere word stickers on metal-rimmed tags; attach to patterned paper strip with safety pins. Stamp date.

Amy Warren, Tyler, Texas

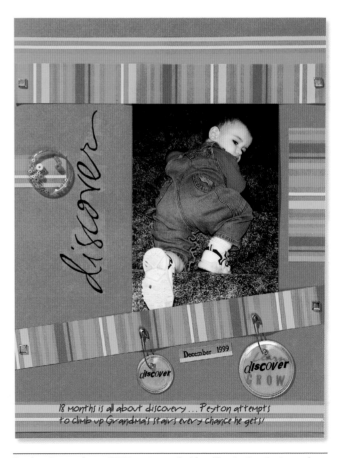

Supplies: Patterned paper/KI Memories; word stickers/Creative Imaginations; rub-on word transfer, date stamp/Making Memories; red cardstock; metal-rimmed tags; square brads; colored beads; watch crystal; safety pins

Supplies: Metallic cardstock, weather vane stamp/Club Scrap; letter die cuts/QuicKutz; landmark stickers/EK Success; travel definition stamp, postage stamp stamp/Hero Arts; compass stamp/JudiKins; suitcase charm/Darice; brown cardstock; vellum; buttons; embossing powder; metallic rub-ons; chalks; circle punch; wax strings; eyelets

World Traveler

Kathi illustrates the story of her family's transcontinental move with a scanned and printed map as the featured accent paper. Die cut title letters from map paper. Mount on brown cardstock tinted with metallic rub-ons and cut into tag shape; attach eyelets and dimensional passport sticker. Quadruple mount photos on solid cardstock and map paper. Journal on vellum. Stamp postage stamp designs on cardstock; chalk and mount next to dimensional landmark stickers on vellum. Stamp travel definition on vellum; chalk to highlight. Mount journaled stamped and embellished vellum over map paper and attach eyelets. Layer with mesh on brown cardstock; cut into tag shape. Mount metal suitcase charm under mesh at top of left border tag. Attach eyelets; loop wax strings from border tag to title. Stamp round designs on vellum and brown cardstock. Layer round design on vellum behind circle frame punched from metallic cardstock; mount with foam spacers.

Kathi Rerek, Scotch Plains, New Jersey

Timeless Beauty

Keri illustrates one of the moments she would like to lock in time. Mount torn patterned paper over brown cardstock strips on beige cardstock background. Stamp watch design on brown cardstock; secure behind photo with spiral clip. Slide large photo under torn patterned paper edge. Layer cardboard, cork, torn and walnut ink-stained cardstock, burlap, and watch face for accent. Make photo image transfer by adhering packing tape firmly over desired photo copied image; rub over back of photo. Submerge in water for a minute or two. Gently rub off paper leaving the image on the sticky side of the tape; dry. Mount translucent tape image on top of textured accent and tie with jute string. Stamp title word. Adhere letter tag stickers and tie fibers.

Keri Key, Burlington, North Carolina

Supplies: Patterned paper, spiral clip, watch face/7 Gypsies; letter tag stickers/EK Success; letter stamps/Hero Arts; watch stamp/Rubber Stampede; brown and beige cardstocks; cardboard; cork; fibers; jute string; burlap; packing tape; walnut ink; brown ink

Whale Watching

Joanna documents an ocean adventure with hidden journaling and an enlarged photo of her favorite shipmate. Lightly sand pre-made photo border. Slice border and mount at top and bottom of brown patterned background. Enlarge one photo and add text with photo-editing software. Print quote and journaling (hidden) on brown cardstock. Cut quote into strip; lightly ink edges. Create hidden journaling block by cutting cardstock 2¼" longer than text on the left side; score and fold to create a flap. Mount photo on flap; secure flap with Velcro on back of photo and on journaling block. Cover one slide mount with patterned paper; stamp name. Punch holes in one corner of each slide mount; string fiber and mount along photo border. Secure slide mounts on page with foam spacers. Embellish with button and small sea star.

Joanna Bolick, Black Mountain, North Carolina
Poem: William Rose Benét

Supplies: Patterned paper/7 Gypsies; letter stamps/PSX Design; brown cardstock; black and burgundy inks; patterned paper; fibers; slide mounts; button; sea star; pre-made photo border; sandpaper; Velcro

Modern Primitive

Mary-Catherine emphasizes the savage nature of her uncivilized little guy on a primitive layout. Stamp background design on brown cardstock background. Mount primitive designs cut from wrapping paper. Mat photo on green cardstock with torn edges. Stamp and emboss letters on blue patterned paper with gold embossing powder. Cut around letters and outline shapes with pen before mounting as title.

Mary-Catherine Kropinski, Maple Ridge, British Columbia, Canada

Supplies: Letter stamps/Stamp Craft; background stamp/Hot Potatoes; patterned paper/(source unknown); brown and green cardstocks; wrapping paper; tiki buttons; gold embossing powder

Recording Your Child's Growth on Pages

Growth charts, pediatrician reports, handprints and other pieces of memorabilia and creative displays of photos can document the way your baby changes over time. One minute he's unable to lift his head and the next, or so it seems, he's striding off on his own. Find inspiration for spreads (pages 70-73) that offer perspective and celebrate your child's progress.

The Hands of Time

Andrea documents the growth of her son with photos and clay hand impressions. Layer transparency over matted patterned paper background. Attach eyelets at background corners; secure watch hand under lower left corner eyelet. String fibers through eyelets across top and bottom of page. Adhere typewriter letters, metal letter tiles and board game letter tiles over fibers. Mount watch charm. Journal on blue cardstock. Wrap journaled strips over one corner of matted photo. Tear ends of large strips before mounting on page. Stamp hands on ceramic tiles. Make additional prints as child grows. Secure handprints and large eyelets pressed in polymer clay; mount clock hands.

Andrea Lyn Vetten-Marley, Aurora, Colorado

Supplies: Patterned paper/Design Originals; printed transparency/Creative Imaginations; game letter tiles; metal letter tiles/Making Memories; typewriter letters/K & Co.; hand stamp/Inkadinkado; fibers; clock hands/Crafts. Etc.; clock charm/7 Gypsies; polymer clay; blue cardstock; large and small eyelets

Miracle

Rachel utilizes graduated colors in subtle tones for a dimensional look that doesn't require 3-D elements. Colored single-tone photos can be reproduced with photo editing software or by photocopying with a single color at a reduced color saturation. Mat small photos on black cardstock. If you can't find graduated color paper, make your own with swipes of colored chalks or stamping with a graduated color pad; blend colors together with a sponge or fingertips. Horizontally layer strips of monochromatic cardstock on graduated color background. Double mat large photo on black cardstock and distressed colored cardstock. Print title and part of journaling on colored cardstock; crop into squares. Print balance of title on transparency.

Rachel Dickson, Calgary, Alberta, Canada

Supplies; Black and colored cardstocks; chalk; transparency

DOCUMENTING BABY'S GROWTH

All of those "firsts" in your baby's life are important because they mark progress as he grows and learns. Each baby step is worth celebrating. Make sure you record and scrapbook all of the following special milestones:

First time he lifts his head on his own

Rolled over	Drank from a cup	Took a step	First haircut
Smiled	Ate solid food	First words	First birthday
Laughed	Was given a bath	First game of patty-cake	First haircut
Scooted	Rode in a swing	First tooth	First Christmas
Sat up unsupported	Pulled himself to his feet	First illness	First Halloween costume
Crawled	Climbed out of his crib	First trip to the park or zoo	First song

Growing in Tandem

Michelle created a fun printed and stitched statistical chart containing 18 months' worth of information about her twins. Ink edges of blue cardstock. Tear patterned paper and mount at bottom of cardstock. Tear a narrow strip of walnut ink-stained cardstock for title strip; mount near top of page. Print title words on rust and brown cardstocks and silhouette cut. Add crystal lacquer; mount over mesh on title strip. Double mat photos with red and blue cardstocks and torn cork; brush gold patina on torn edges and mount on title strip. Journal on blue cardstock and mat on walnut ink-stained cardstock; tear bottom edges. Double mat color photo with red and blue cardstocks; tear mat edges. Print growth chart on transparency. Mount on cork and tear edge; melt gold foil on torn edge with hot foil pen. Apply gold patina around other three edges of cork. Hand stitch along chart lines through cork and transparency with black, red and blue embroidery threads. Print definition, chart and photo captions, and dates on walnut ink-stained cardstock. Crop all text blocks and ink edges. Mount definition at right side of page. Mat height/weight text on pieces of torn cork brushed with gold patina and mount on both sides of chart. Mount printed chart information on top of stitched transparency and months/dates under chart.

Michelle Pendleton, Colorado Springs, Colorado

Supplies: Patterned paper/K & Co.; paper lacquer/JudiKins; gold patina/Amaco; watermark ink/Tsukineko; gold foil, hot foil pen/Staedtler; blue, rust, red and brown cardstocks; cork; mesh; walnut ink; embroidery floss; transparency

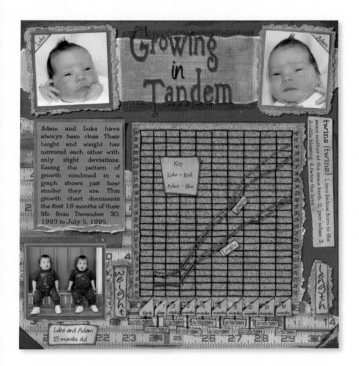

Where Has Time Gone?

Kristin marks the passage of time with photos showing how her infant has become a fun-loving toddler. Mount matted photos on layered sliced and torn cardstock strips; curl torn edges. Journal on white cardstock; mat on tan cardstock and embellish with fibers and watch charm. Handcut printed title from white and tan cardstocks.

Kristin Baxter, Valdosta, Georgia

Supplies: Charm/www.Scrapsahoy.com; white and tan cardstocks; fibers; chalk

Blossom

A cheerful border of first-year photos provides a visual record of Kelly's daughter's changing looks. Vertically mount a narrow strip of green patterned paper on left edge of white cardstock background. Mount cropped photos behind preprinted paper slide frames. Vertically and horizontally mount photo slide frames, leaving space between each slide. Cut a piece of yellow patterned paper; mount, leaving space between paper and slide frames. Mat four photos on one piece of white cardstock. Mount a narrow strip of pink paper just inside top edge of page. Mount a narrow patterned paper strip over left edge of yellow patterned paper. Print monthly growth information on transparency; cut to fit on top of preprinted tags and mount. Lightly brush edges of tags with black ink pad; mount on border strip with colored eyelets. Ink edges of dimensional letter stickers, colored metal flowers and preprinted circles. Assemble floral embellishments with metal flowers mounted on circles with colored eyelets. Adhere letter stickers and flower embellishment for one letter "o" in title. Mount remaining embellishments on title strip, left border strip and over bottom right corner of matted photos. Adhere numbers and letter stickers on photos and slide frames.

Kelly Angard, Highlands Ranch, Colorado

Supplies: Patterned paper, preprinted tags, circles and slide mounts/KI Memories; letter, number stickers/Creative Imaginations/Making Memories; metal flowers/Carolee's Creations; white cardstock; eyelets; black ink pad

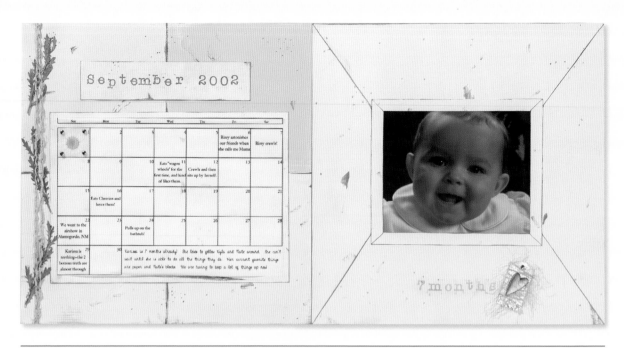

Supplies: Patterned paper/Rusty Pickle; letter stamps/Close To My Heart; plastic window/Chatterbox; metal tag, pewter heart/Making Memories; watermark ink/Tsukineko; pink paper; tan cardstock; vellum; fiber; beads; silver brads; dried flowers; ink; pink chalk

September 2002

Maureen records her daughter's growth with a detailed calendar page. Print calendar page with developmental milestones and journaling on vellum. Mount calendar on ivory paper with inked edges. Layer plastic window over dried flower; attach with brads. Stamp month and year on pink paper strip; ink edges. Mount dried leaves at left side of page; wrap fibers over leaves and secure. For the right-hand page, create "dimensional wooden frame" with distressed patterned paper sliced, inked and reassembled. Draw ruled pencil lines from each corner to center of page. Slice into sections along pencil lines; ink edges of sliced sections. Reassemble sections on tan cardstock. Slice four ½" strips of pink paper for photo frame using the steps described above; cut ends of strips on an angle. Stamp age with watermark ink; brush with pink chalk. Embellish metal tag with pewter heart, beads and fiber; attach to page with brad.

Maureen Spell, Carlsbad, New Mexico

Bear With Me

Susan records her son's growth by taking photos each month of him next to a large stuffed bear. Print journaling and balance of title on blue patterned paper; layer with pieces of tan patterned paper and handmade cardstock on blue patterned paper background. Mount ruler stickers on page. Stamp title on large tag and age on small tags with watermark ink. Adhere bear stickers on large tag; tie all tags with ribbon. Layer small tags with photos on page. Adhere typewriter letter stickers.

Susan Cyrus, Broken Arrow, Oklahoma

Supplies: Patterned paper/Anna Griffin/K & Co./Karen Foster Design; handmade cardstock/(source unknown); letter stamps/Hero Arts; letter stickers, ruler stickers/EK Success; bear stickers/K & Co.; tags/2DYE4; watermark ink/Tsukineko; red ribbon

Two Months

Jennifer records her son's growth on pages monthly. Begin by slicing two ¼" strips of orange cardstock, two ³⁄₁₆" strips of light blue cardstock, two ½" strips of both yellow cardstock and patterned paper, and one ¼" strip of navy blue cardstock. Mount orange strips at top and bottom of navy blue cardstock background and light blue strips just inside of orange strips. Print journaling list on green cardstock; mount buttons as bullet points. Mount photo and journaling list side by side near top of page; layer narrow dark blue strip along right photo edge. Mount patterned paper and yellow cardstock strips above and below photo/journaling. Print and silhouette cut title from green cardstock; mount on yellow strip.

Jennifer Bourgeault, Macomb Township, Michigan

Supplies: Patterned paper/Chatterbox; orange, light and navy blue, yellow, green cardstocks; buttons

Six Months

Slice a ⅝" and a 1¼" strip of patterned paper; two ¼" strips of red cardstock and one ¼" strip of white cardstock. Mount a red strip near top of green cardstock background. Print and silhouette cut title from white cardstock; mount under red strip. Print journaling list on green cardstock; mount buttons as bullet points. Mount photo and journaling list side by side at top of page; layer other red strip along right edge of photo. Mount ⅝" strip of patterned paper above photo/journaling and 1¼" patterned paper strip below photo/journaling. Layer white strip along top of patterned paper strip at bottom of page.

Jennifer Bourgeault, Macomb Township, Michigan

Supplies: Patterned paper/Chatterbox; red. white and green cardstocks; buttons

One

Slice a 1" strip of mustard cardstock, a 4" strip of green cardstock and a ⅜" strip of white cardstock. Tear one edge of green cardstock; layer with white strip and mount at bottom of navy blue cardstock background. Double mat photo on green and mustard cardstocks. Print journaling list on white cardstock; layer on page over torn vellum strips and attach with eyelets. Highlight words with colored chalks. Print and silhouette cut title word from white cardstock; layer over mustard cardstock strip mounted near top of page. Tear five small squares from mustard cardstock; layer with printed and silhouette-cut numbers over white strip.

Jennifer Bourgeault, Macomb Township, Michigan

Supplies: Mustard, green, white and blue cardstocks; vellum; colored eyelets; chalk

The Sweetest Flower of Spring

Ribbon and embroidered trim lead the viewer's eye toward photos of Andrea's daughter. Diagonally string ribbon and embroidered flower border across an embossed cardstock background. Wrap ribbon ends around cardstock and adhere. Mount pink bow over ribbon intersections. Double and triple mat photos with off-white cardstock and torn mulberry paper. Print title and journaling on vellum; tear edges and layer with photos over and under ribbon. Mat green embossed cardstock background on dark green cardstock; whip stitch edges with beaded embroidery thread. Pierce holes around both the dark green and embossed cardstocks. Add four pink beads with each stitch. Tie pieces of embroidery thread into small bows; mount at each corner. Complete page with metal embellishments; stitch metal flower charm to page under ribbon bow; attach metal flower eyelets.

Andrea Lyn Vetten-Marley, Aurora, Colorado

Supplies: Embossed cardstock/K & Co.; metal flower eyelets/Making Memories; flower charm/Simply Charmed; off-white and dark green cardstocks; mulberry paper; vellum; pink beads; flower trim; embroidery floss; pink ribbon

Sweet Baby Girl

Candi's sense of style is rubbing off on her baby girl! Cut pink patterned paper to fit vertical half of pink background cardstock and mount. Layer second patterned paper square over background. Mount textured ribbon across page; secure. Insert preprinted words into conchos for title; mount near photos. Print journaling on white cardstock. Mount flower charm in bottom right corner.

Candi Gershon, Fishers, Indiana

Supplies: Patterned paper/Anna Griffin/Magenta; preprinted words, conchos/Scrapworks; metal flower charm/(source unknown); pink and white cardstocks; ribbon

Clap for Joy

Shelleyrae features a delightful photo that needs no embellishment! Re-create this computer-generated page by matting an enlarged photo on black cardstock. Print title and journaling on transparency and layer over enlarged photo.

Shelleyrae Cusbert, South Windsor, Australia

Supplies: Black cardstock; transparency

Tutti Frutti Summer Cutie

Debra creates a feminine layout that speaks to a little girl, without being cutesy. Mat patterned paper on pink cardstock for background. Rub tan and pink ink on ivory cardstock, crumple and flatten. Write title on crumpled cardstock; tear edges. Mount one title word over pink raffia strip with foam spacers. Laminate dried flowers and silhouette cut; mount on raffia strip. Mat photo on pink cardstock; mount above text sticker on embossed paper strip. Layer vellum journaling block over torn cardstock; journal. Mount sentiment stone on text sticker matted with distressed cardstock. Wrap fibers around bottom of page; mount balance of title words over fibers with foam spacers. Add pink jewels on vellum and attach nailhead on text sticker. Secure swirl clips on embossed cardstock and edge of page.

Debra Beagle, Milton, Tennessee

Supplies: Patterned paper/Cut-It-Up; embossed paper/Solum World; text stickers/Memories Complete; gold swirl clips/Making Memories; sentiment stone/Robert Schumann; pink and ivory cardstocks; vellum; fibers; raffia; dried flowers; gold nailhead; pink jewels; laminate

MY BABY TAUGHT ME

My baby taught me that the little moments in time are the most important and they will stay etched in your memory forever. It's the very moment she came out of my body, not the entire labor process. It's the first time she wrapped her little hand around my finger and held on tight. It's when she can sense that I'm having a bad day and she looks up at me with those big blue eyes and smiles. It's the quietness you hear as you hold her after everyone else in the room has tried to calm her.

Holly Simoni, Madrid, Iowa

Summer Perfection

Vanessa focuses on her daughter's memorable summer sensations with a torn vellum frame highlighting grass on a tiny toe. Mount sliced patterned paper on pink cardstock background; ink edges. Mat photo on pink cardstock; ink edges. Use template to create title word; stamp other title word on pink cardstock and ink edges. Mount metal-rimmed tag with torn vellum around photo detail. Layer printed circle tags on metal-rimmed tags; dangle from ribbon wrapped across page and tied into a bow.

Vanessa Spady, Virginia Beach, Virginia

Supplies: Patterned paper, printed circle tags/KI Memories; lettering template/Wordsworth; letter stamps/Stamp Craft; pink cardstock; vellum; metal-rimmed tags; ribbon; ink

Crisp, Sweet, Fresh

Jessie focuses in on her son's first "taste" of summer. Slice narrow strips of patterned text paper and black cardstock; tear one edge. Ink torn edges; layer and mount at bottom of brown cardstock background. Slice a strip of gold cardstock; mount near left side of page. Layer photos and black cardstock on page. Ink edges of small tag; stamp two words and write one word. Cut large tag from black cardstock; crumple and flatten. Craft handmade reinforcement from brown cardstock to look like purchased tag and punch hole. Write words on twill fabric scrap; ink edges and mount on tag with square brads. Mount title silver letter stickers on black tag. Tie both tags with ribbon and layer at top of page. Mount definition strip with inked edges over enlarged photo; attach square brad. Mount ribbon near bottom of page. Stamp date above ribbon. Journal.

Jessie Baldwin, Las Vegas, Nevada

Supplies: Patterned paper, walnut ink/7 Gypsies/KI Memories; silver letter stamps/Hero Arts; date stamp, definition/Making Memories; black, gold and brown cardstocks; twill fabric; tag; square brads; ribbon; ink

Water Fun

Simple embellishments, minimal journaling and closely cropped photos allow Michele's son to shine on her layout. Layer two photos over torn patterned paper background. Slice large photo into squares; reassemble as mosaic leaving space between each piece. Journal on white cardstock; layer under vellum. Curl wire, string with letter beads for title and feed through attached eyelets. Secure at back of page.

Michele Tisler, Madison, Alabama

Supplies: Patterned papers/Provo Craft; letter beads/Westrim; white cardstock, vellum; eyelets; wire; eyelets

Bluebonnet

It's easy to see how much Jennifer's son enjoyed this field of flowers. Layer pieces of colored cardstock and mesh for a color-blocked background. Cut off tops of metal letter charms; layer on colored cardstock scraps for title. Rub on white word transfer. Stamp swirl and ivy designs on white cardstock; slice, ink edges and reassemble on green cardstock. Journal on white cardstock; attach flower charm with small brad. Mat one photo on white cardstock; mount metal frame over cropped photo.

Jennifer Brookover, San Antonio, Texas

Supplies: Metal letters, rub-on word/Making Memories; ivy stamp/ Denami Designs; small swirl/A Stamp in the Hand; big swirl/JudiKins; flower charm/Charming Pages; purple, white and green cardstocks; mesh; metal frame; brad

Moments of Solitude

Jessie selects photos that catch her eye and move her spirit. Print journaling on mustard cardstock background. Slice a ⅞" and 1¾" strip of patterned vellum and a 2" strip of a patterned paper. Layer the 2" and ⅞" patterned strips at left side of page. Mount enlarged photo above patterned vellum strip. Mount smaller photo near journaling. Rub on word transfer for title at top of page over border strips. Mount watch over punched black cardstock square. Adhere definition sticker with black cardstock square under enlarged photo.

Jessie Baldwin, Las Vegas, Nevada

Supplies: Patterned papers/Provo Craft; letter beads/Westrim; white cardstock, vellum; eyelets; wire; eyelets

Your Favorite Hat

Amber displays photos of her son in his favorite hat on a top-rate page. Journal on vellum; layer over patterned paper and mount on coordinating patterned paper background with small brads. Mat photo on patterned paper. Adhere title letter stickers. Frame small photos with slide mounts covered with patterned paper. Mount of right side of page.

Amber Crosby, Houston, Texas

Supplies: Patterned paper/Chatterbox; letter stickers/Colorbök; vellum; slide mounts; copper brads

MY BABY TAUGHT ME

It's OK to go slow and enjoy all of the little things. I've always been in a rush trying to cram as many things as possible into my day. When you have a baby, that all goes right out the window! I now take my time walking from the car to the store. It gives my son a chance to check out all of the cars. I now sit out in the back yard doing nothing but watching my son. There's nothing more peaceful than watching a happy, content toddler discover and play!

Kristin Baxter, Houston, Texas

That I had patience I didn't know I had.

Valerie Salmon, Carmel, Indiana

La La La

Monique celebrates the joyful babbling that marked her baby's early stage of language development. Mount torn patterned paper and cardstock strips on brown cardstock background. Wrap corner with tied twine. Mat photos; layer with ephemera. Adhere letter stickers. Personalize labels with label-maker; mount on page.

Monique McLean, Pleasant Grove, Alabama

Supplies: Patterned paper, letter stickers, ephemera/ Me & My Big Ideas; label words/ Dymo; brown cardstock; twine

Patton Bertsch

It was a bittersweet moment for Jennifer when she realized her baby was growing up. Cut patterned paper into desired sizes; sand edges. Mat on coordinating solid paper and sand again. Layer matted paper with photos on ivory cardstock background; swipe cardstock edges with green ink pad. Mount photo behind preprinted distressed frame; position bookplate over stamped date and attach with brads. Affix gold photo corners to frame and mount on page with foam spacers. Brush edges of definition stickers with colored chalks and place randomly on page. Mount buttons.

Jennifer Bertsch, Tallahassee, Florida

Supplies: Patterned paper/Mustard Moon; definition stickers/ Making Memories; preprinted distressed frame/My Mind's Eye; date stamp; ivory cardstock; green ink; gold photo corners; bookplate; buttons; brads; chalk; sandpaper

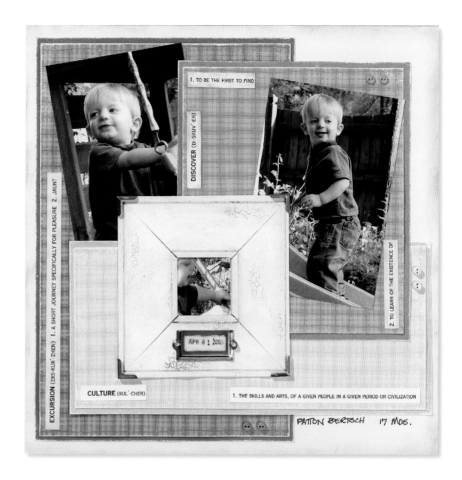

Concentration

The delights of discovery are alluring at any age, including the realization that one has feet. Using a craft knife and ruler, slice windows into red cardstock squares, creating ½" frames. Mount mesh behind cut windows; layer with photos on tan background cardstock. Attach metal phrase eyelet in one window. Print title and name/ age on white cardstock; crop and paper clip to photos. String fasteners on wire; diagonally wrap across page; secure. Secure fasteners over cropped photos.

Robin Hohenstern, Brooklyn Park, Minnesota

Supplies: Date stamp, metal phrase eyelet/Making Memories; red, tan and white cardstocks; wire; mesh; clips; paper clips

Discover Sand

Jessie journals her baby's fascination with sand. Tear a piece of patterned paper; layer on gray cardstock background with pieces of mesh, handmade paper and gray and brown cardstocks. Crop enlarged photo; slice window for metal plaque and mount on page. Attach brads over mesh at top of page. Write journaling on vellum; tear left edge and mount at bottom of page. String letter charms on embroidery floss; wrap thread around page and secure. Adhere letters to page. Rub-on word transfers for title.

Jessie Baldwin, Las Vegas, Nevada

Supplies: Patterned paper/Creative Imaginations; handmade paper/Magenta; letter charms, rub-on words, brads, metal seashell accent/Making Memories; gray cardstock; vellum; mesh; embroidery floss

The Reluctant Cowboy

A cowboy comes to life on this kick-up-your-boots page. Adhere a brown patterned paper block with sanded edges on background patterned paper. Distress edges of photo and mount on paper block. Journal on vellum; tear top edge and mount with cross stitches. Print title on patterned paper, crop and stitch to page. Finish title with letter stamps; crop letters, mat and mount. Embellish with punched strip and hemp lasso. Finish with journaled note inserted in envelope decorated with circular tag and snaps.

Erica Hernandez, Fresno State, California

Supplies: Patterned paper/Chatterbox; stamp/PSX Design; envelope, letter stamp/Foofala; frame/Chatterbox; cardstock; tacks; twine; brad; ink

When on Life's Trail...

Linda creates a relaxed layout with a faux stitched leather patch and denim belt loop tag pull. Hand paint photos with photo-painting oils; chalk and ink edges. Layer cut and torn patterned papers with chalked and inked edges; stitch. Roll torn edges. Cut tag from tan cardstock; paint and ink edges. Attach metal frame over printed word with brads. Layer torn and chalked patterned papers; cut and fold into tag envelope. Mount large photo over tag envelope and tag; attach metal letter eyelet. Adhere denim belt loop on tag and page; wrap belt loop around edges of page. Stamp date on belt loop; stitch buttons. Print quote and caption on transparency; attach brads. Mat small photo; stitch along right edge of page. Create the look of a leather label by covering ivory cardstock with amber paint; ink edges. Crumple and flatten; ink and adhere to same-sized chipboard. Print text on layers of torn and chalked patterned papers; adhere over chipboard. Coat with decoupage glue matte finish; let dry. Stitch around edges.

Linda Albrecht, Saint Peter, Minnesota

Supplies: Patterned papers/DMD/Provo Craft; metal letter/K & Co.; metal tag/Making Memories; chipboard; transparency; tan and ivory cardstocks; jeans; brads; amber paint; chalk; photo painting oils

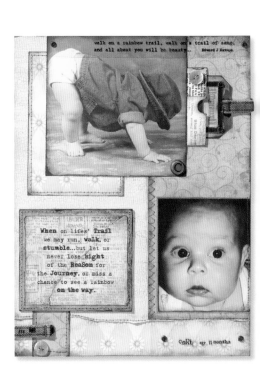

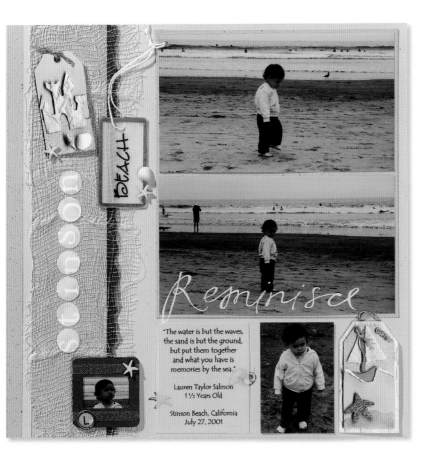

Stinson Beach

Valerie enhances the serenity of the beach with a gauze "netting" and ocean-themed embellishments. Layer left side border with strips of light blue, tan and blue cardstock, on light blue cardstock background. Wrap gauze bandage over border strips and secure. Adhere title letter stickers on gauze. Mat two photos on one piece of tan cardstock; punch small hole at top left corner. Adhere sticker word on metal-rimmed tag and tie to matted photo; secure tag on netting and embellish with seashell buttons. Add texture to colored slide mount with sand adhered to strips of strong double-sided tape; embellish with sea star button and page pebble mounted over letter sticker. Mount slide over cropped photo with foam spacers. Rub white word transfer on one photo. Print journaling on tan vellum; mount over seashell stickers adhered to page. Punch hole in preprinted tags; tie with jute string. Mount at top of border and at bottom of page with foam spacers.

Valerie Salmon, Carmel, Indiana
Quote: Author unknown

Supplies: Letter stickers/Creative Imaginations; rub-on words, page pebble/Making Memories; sticker word/C-Thru Ruler; typewriter letter, preprinted tags/EK Success; seashell stickers/Frances Meyer; colored slide mount/Foofala; blue, light blue and tan cardstocks; jute string; metal-rimmed tag; seashell buttons; gauze bandage; sand

You Stand Here...

Softly torn and layered vellum strips enhance the serene atmosphere of this page. Mount photo corners on patterned paper background before matting on black cardstock. Mat photos on white cardstock; mount with photo corners. Print title, photo caption and journaling on vellum; tear sides and mount title over photo. Layer photo caption with sea star over vellum strip and glassine envelope. Mount journaling over layers of torn cardstock; mat on black cardstock and embellish with faux wax seal. Attach binder clips.

Carrie O'Donnell, Newburyport, Massachusetts

Supplies: Patterned paper, faux wax shell seal/Creative Imaginations; sea star sticker/EK Success; black cardstock; vellum; glassine envelope; photo corners; binder clips

FOUR

. the whole world .
is his hand

He's been bathed, fed, burped and cuddled by Mommy
What else could a baby want? Continuing Warmth? Safety?
Tenderness? Love? All right here in

D A D D Y'S

H A N D .

Wyatt (1 week old) takes a rest.

Let's Shoot Some Black-and-White

The mere thought of a baby conjures up an aurora of color—the shell pink of a blushed cheek, tousled golden curls, the pastel lavenders of a frilled nursery, the flaming red of a first-Christmas outfit and buoyantly illustrated picture books, a chicken-yellow blankie loved paper thin. And yet more and more scrapbookers are choosing to photograph their babies in black-and-white or ambered sepia tones. Time-less black-and-white images reflect a simpler time of grace, relying on the play of light and shadow to call the eye to the beauty of an infant's perfect pores, the folds behind a chubby knee or the shell-like grace of a tiny ear. Scrapbook black-and-white or sepia photos of your baby on monochromatic pages for a powerfully elegant spread or select vibrant back-ground papers that make your photos pop.

I'd like to be played as a child by Natalie Wood. I'd have some romantic scenes as Audrey Hepburn and have gritty black-and-white scenes as Patricia Neal.

Gloria Steinem

Supplies: Embossed silver stickers/Colorbök; shades of blue cardstock, white cardstock; yarn; beads; flower sequins; silver nailheads; chalk; crystal lacquer

Angel of Mine

The shine of sprinkled metallic beads pale in comparison to the radiant glow of Leah's son. Assemble monochromatic color-blocked background with torn, sliced and chalked pieces of cardstock in shades of blue. Mat photo; tear and chalk edges. Print title on white cardstock; silhouette cut and add crystal lacquer. Embellish embossed stickers with nailheads, flower sequins and colored beads. Wrap yarn across page; secure one end under nailhead and other end at back of page. Mount beads as border design and randomly on the page.

Leah LaMontagne, Las Vegas, Nevada

SHOOTING BETTER BLACK-AND-WHITE PHOTOS

Keep the following pointers in mind in order to shoot the very best black-and-white pictures possible:

- Black-and-white photos are best when the elements in the shot contrast dramatically. If you are taking pictures of your baby, make sure her skin tone and her outfit are very different colors (a dark outfit on a fair child etc.), and make sure that the background environment contrasts with both your baby and her outfit.

- Lighting is very important when shooting a superior black-and-white picture. Not enough light will result in a muddy picture with poor contrast. Too much or too direct of a light source will result in dramatic and often unattractive shadows.

- Avoid busy environments and backgrounds when shooting black-and-white. They will draw focus from your baby's image.

- Move in tight on your baby's image to decrease conflicting background clutter.

- Consider using window light when shooting black-and-white photos.

- Identify those moments that are best suited for black-and-white including portraits. Shots that include highly textured objects such as blankets and teddy bears work well. However the moods of activities including birthdays, holidays and sporting events can often be better captured using color film.

Remember that color photos can be printed in black-and-white or sepia by most photo processors. If you have a color photo that you wish to scrapbook in black-and-white, take the negative to your photo lab and ask for a black-and-white or sepia print.

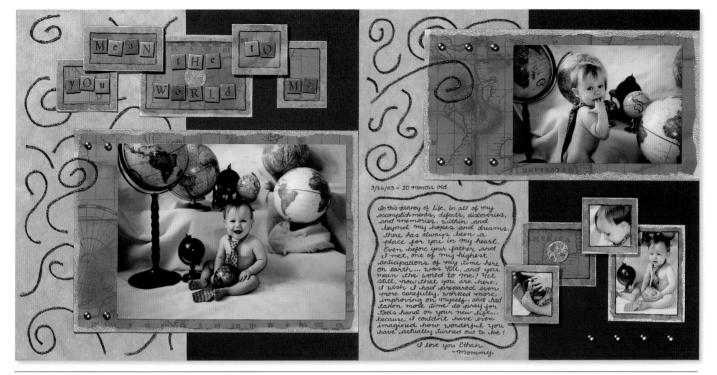

Supplies: Patterned paper/EK Success/Karen Foster Design/Mustard Moon; metal letter tiles/Making Memories; earth stamp/(source unknown); black cardstock; pen; embroidery floss; gold nailheads; silver embossing powder; ink; photo-tinting markers

You Mean the World to Me

Leah expresses feelings she hopes will accompany her son on his life journeys. Mount patterned paper cut to fit vertical half of black cardstock background. Draw swirls on patterned paper; trace with liquid adhesive and mount embroidery floss. Mat large photos on patterned paper; ink edges and emboss with silver embossing powder. Mount metal letter tiles and stamp world with silver ink on patterned paper. Cut frames for title blocks, small photos and stamped image from brown patterned paper; outline inside edge of frames with pen. Ink outside edges of frames and emboss with silver embossing powder; layer on page with foam spacers. Journal. Attach nailheads.

Leah LaMontagne, Las Vegas, Nevada

Jack Frost

A cleverly hidden journaling block invites interaction with Andrea's bold page. Mat enlarged photo on black cardstock background. Print title on white cardstock; silhouette cut. Press cut title on watermark pad; sprinkle with silver embossing powder and heat to set; repeat. Create a flip-up title border to hide journaling. Mount gingham ribbon 4" from top of patterned paper; glue metal-rimmed tag on ribbon with a strong adhesive and mount charm on tag. Horizontally score blue patterned paper ¼" from top edge; fold to create a flap. Apply adhesive on scored edge of patterned paper so it can lift to reveal journaling block; mount on page. Mount embossed title on border; stamp words under title. Layer embroidered snowflake over mesh triangle. Slice a 3¾" piece of both patterned vellum and white cardstock; layer vellum over white cardstock and then mount under lift-up flap. Journal.

Andrea Hautala, Olympia, Washington

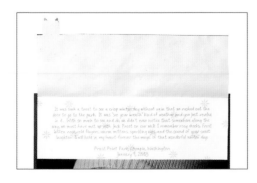

Supplies: Patterned paper/Sweetwater; patterned vellum/Colorbök; silver charm/Rhode Island Bead & Components; letter stamps/Hero Arts; black and white cardstocks; silver embossing powder; ribbon; wire mesh; metal-rimmed tag; embroidered snowflake

Supplies: *Patterned papers, stickers/Daisy D's; letter stamps/PSX Design; letter stickers, metal letters, phrase eyelet, metal-rimmed tags, buckle/Making Memories; date stamp; white and blue cardstocks; blue vellum; tags; ribbon; nails; button; photo corners; circle punch; yellow acrylic paint; ink*

My Precious Boy

Valerie captured the essence of her busy baby on a creatively embellished page. Cut patterned text paper to fit horizontally across spread; mount over gingham patterned paper. Slice a strip of yellow patterned paper; mount across middle of pages. Print descriptive words on white cardstock; slice into strip; mount near top of pages. For left page, mat photo on blue cardstock; adhere sticker border under photo. Ink edges of tags; add stickers, button and fiber. Mount photo on page with photo corners. Print caption and journaling on vellum. Slice out center of metal-rimmed tag. Mount tag over caption. Stamp one title word and adhere letter stickers on preprinted tags; ink edges. Stitch small tag and blue vellum strip on page. Tie remaining tag with blue ribbon and mount with foam spacers. Paint metal letter charms and metal phrase eyelet with yellow acrylic paint; assemble letters for title on blue vellum strip. Mount phrase eyelet under photo. On right page, frame photo with descriptive word strips. Feed ribbon through metal buckle; wrap around framed photo. Print definition on white cardstock; ink edges and attach square nails. Layer over matted photo and mount with foam spacers. Stamp date next to matted photo. Adhere stickers on white cardstock; single and double mat on solid and patterned papers. Tie ribbon through punched holes and mount. Stitch journaling block on page. Stamp letters on preprinted circle tags; mount.

Valerie Salmon, Carmel, Indiana

Unison

Erica remembers napping with her baby on his stormy and colicky days. Print title and journaling on patterned background paper. Sand edges of photo; layer over embroidered paper and mount to background paper.

Erica Hernandez, Fresno, California

Supplies: *Patterned paper/Sweetwater; embroidered paper/Jennifer Collection; sandpaper*

Supplies: Patterned paper/Design Originals; letter stickers/EK Success; metal letter charms/Making Memories; tag/7 Gypsies; tan and brown cardstocks; fibers; eyelets; date stamp; chalk

Our Favorite Things About You

Ellen uses monochromatic color and minimal embellishment to focus the eye on her daughter. Double mat enlarged photo on tan cardstock and patterned paper; tear edges of first mat. Mount on brown cardstock background. Adhere letter stickers on walnut ink-stained tag; stamp date. Wrap page with fibers and tie to tag. Mount photos along top of right page. Print title and journaling on patterned vellum; trim and chalk. Mat on tan cardstock. Mount metal letter charms to complete title. Attach to page with eyelets; string fibers through eyelets.

Ellen Hargrove, Jenks, Oklahoma

One Year Old

Kimberly adds a splash of color to a monochromatic page. Stitch black patterned paper with torn edge over gray patterned paper strips; mount on black cardstock background. Gently curl torn edge and secure with brads. Adhere title letter stickers. Tear bottom edge of photo; layer over colored block photo border. Embellish photo with black mesh, leather/grommet trim and button. Cut tag from gray cardstock; chalk and zigzag stitch edges. Adhere letter stickers on small chalked tags; layer over torn patterned paper. Stitch button to black cardstock scrap; layer on tag with mesh. Attach antique brads on lettered tags.

Kimberly Delong, Fremont, Michigan
Photo: JC Penney Portrait, Musk, Michigan

Supplies: Patterned paper/C-Thru Ruler/Paper Patch; letter stickers/Creative Imaginations/EK Success; photo border/Creative Imaginations; black cardstock; mesh; leather/grommet trim; silver and gold brads; buttons

Emily

Rebecca softens a striped background by rubbing sandpaper over cardstock strips. Slice strips of cream and pink cardstock of varied widths; rub strips with sandpaper. Mount on white cardstock background, leaving space between strips. Mat photos on white cardstock. Stamp title letters in warm silver embossing powder. Let cool; cut into tiles. Stamp and emboss descriptive words and date.

Rebecca Cooper, Claresholm, Alberta, Canada

Supplies: Letter stamps/PSX Design; date stamp; cream, pink and white cardstocks; silver embossing powder; sandpaper

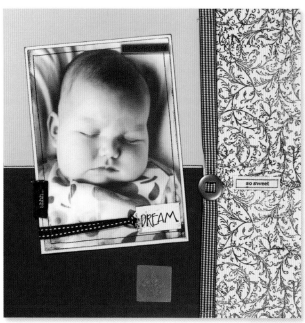

Dream

Janet transforms a photo of her daughter into a work of art by printing it on canvas. Cut black cardstock to fit half of pink cardstock background; stitch border. Stamp fleur-de-lis design; heat emboss with silver embossing powder. Stamp light pink cardstock with toile design; heat emboss with black embossing powder. String buckle on ribbon; mount. Mount pink embroidered tag. Print photo on canvas made for inkjet printers; stitch and ink edges. Mat on pink cardstock. Brush pink acrylic paint over metal tag. Rub with sandpaper; rub on word transfer. Tie ribbon to tag, attach star charm with jump ring and mount on photo. Attach staple; stick t-pin through embroidered tag. Affix metal phrase eyelet.

Janet Hopkins, Frisco, Texas

Supplies: Canvas photo paper/Office Depot; rub-on word, metal phrase eyelet/Making Memories; toile stamp/Stampin' Up!; fleur-de-lis stamp/Hero Arts; star charm/Sam Moon Trading Co.; embroidered tags/Me and My Big Ideas; pink cardstock; metal tag; gingham ribbon; black ribbon; t-pin; staples; silver and black embossing powders; pink acrylic paint

Oh, That Face!

A quick, easy page captures Heather's daughter's antics. Cut patterned paper to fit vertical half of black cardstock background. Mat photo on white cardstock. Print title and journaling on white cardstock; layer over patterned paper square. Adhere small word sticker on punched black cardstock square; mount as part of title with foam spacers. Wrap gingham ribbon across page and tie. Adhere large word stickers.

Heather Preckel, Swannanoa, North Carolina

Supplies: Patterned paper/7 Gypsies; word stickers/Creative Imaginations; black and white cardstocks; ribbon

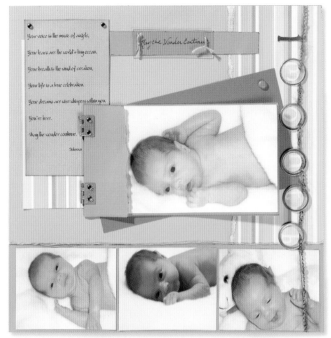

May the Wonder Continue

A new mother conceals loving thoughts under a hinged, matted photo. Tear and chalk patterned paper strip; mount over lavender cardstock background. Mount photos on orange cardstock strip; layer with embroidery floss. Print poem on gold cardstock; ink edges and layer over patterned paper and pink cardstock strip. Write title and draw border on pink strip. Lay plastic microscope slide over title; pierce holes through slide and pink strip. String fibers through holes and tie. Mat photo on pink cardstock. Cut strip of pink cardstock longer than matted photo; tear and ink left edge. Fold edge over matted photo and mount; attach hinges over fold with brads. Layer over purple cardstock; attach red brad. Lift flap and write journaling. Adhere letter stickers on metal-rimmed tags. String metal number and tags on fiber; wrap around page and secure tags.

Keri Key, Burlington, North Carolina

Supplies: Patterned paper/Chatterbox; letter stickers/Creative Imaginations; metal number/ Making Memories; lavender, orange, pink, purple and gold cardstocks; metal-rimmed tags; fibers; embroidery floss; hinges; brads; plastic microscope slide; silver embossing powder; ink; chalk

Brittney's Journal

Vikki creates a safe place for journaling under a hinged cover. Layer patterned paper over black cardstock and mount on burgundy paper background. Attach letter with brad over paper strips on metal-rimmed vellum tag and mesh. Adhere title letter stickers. Mat photo on black cardstock. Adhere number stickers over layered paper strips and mesh. Attach hinges to two pieces of same sized black cardstock with brads. Embellish cover with torn patterned and solid papers; adhere title metal and letter stickers. Mount charms and mesh scrap under watch crystal. Layer and mount silver hearts; tie with ribbon. Journal on white cardstock; cut to fit under embellished cover.

Vikki Hall, Rogers, Arkansas

Supplies: Patterned paper/7 Gypsies/Colorbōk/Honey Cottage/Paper Adventures; letter stickers/Colorbōk/Creative Imaginations/EK Success/Me & My Big Ideas/SEI; metal letters, heart charm/Making Memories; lock and key charm/(source unknown); black cardstock; metal-rimmed tag; mesh; ribbon; brads; hinges; watch crystal

Growing Beauty

Amy adds color and texture to layers of cardstock to offset her daughter's flawless beauty. Slice large window in black cardstock; shade with white ink. Mount patterned paper behind sliced window for background. Double mat photo; distress second mat and lightly ink. String key on ribbon; wrap around double-matted photo and tie. Mount matted photo over framed background, making sure to apply adhesive only around three edges. Slide journaling envelope behind matted photo. Adhere label tape with words along edge of journaling envelope and at bottom of page as part of title. Mount metal letter tiles to complete title.

Amy Howe, Frisco, Texas

Supplies: Patterned paper/Mustard Moon; metal letter tiles/Making Memories; key charm/Jest Charming; black cardstock; pink ribbon; gingham ribbon; label tape; white ink

A Birthmother's Love...

Melodee understands the immense amount of love felt by her son's birthmother. Print title on green patterned paper; layer with torn patterned papers for background; curl torn edges. Adhere tape measure sticker. Mat metal letter tile on patterned paper; mount with printed title. Attach heart eyelet. Print sepia-toned photos on transparency; mount one photo with metal corners. Journal on transparency; layer with torn patterned paper on peach paper. Attach eyelet over punched circle and tie with ribbon. Slip journaled tag behind small matted transparent photo. String metal word tag on sheer ribbon; tie around page and knot ends.

Melodee Langworthy, Rockford, Michigan

Supplies: Patterned papers/Amscan/EK Success/Provo Craft; metal letter tile, metal heart eyelet/Making Memories; metal word tag/K & Co.; transparency; sheer ribbon; metal photo corners

Anna Ward

Cherie designed a stunning title page for her daughter's baby book with ephemera collaged around an engaging photo. Layer and collage ephemera, poem stones and faux stamp over patterned background paper. Print title on mustard cardstock; silhouette cut and mount across top of photo matted with brown cardstock. Mount silver snap letters above photo and faux wax seal at bottom corner. Encase dried flowers between layers of mica; cut into tag shape and outline with gold leafing pen. Attach eyelet, adhere letter stickers and tie with fibers. Secure fibers along top of page. Write date on walnut ink-stained tag; tie with fibers and layer over matted photo. Wrap fibers up over top of page and secure. Write title page information on copper tag using metal embosser. Simulate envelope fastener with small punched circles attached with copper eyelets; wrap with fibers. Mount beads across corners of page.

Cherie Ward, Colorado Springs, Colorado

Supplies: Patterned papers/7 Gypsies/Rusty Pickle; letter stickers/EK Success; metal snap letters/All My Memories; poem stones, faux wax seals, faux stamp/Creative Imaginations; copper tag/Rusty Pickle; fibers; mustard and brown cardstocks; beads; gold leafing pen; mica; miscellaneous ephemera; dried flowers

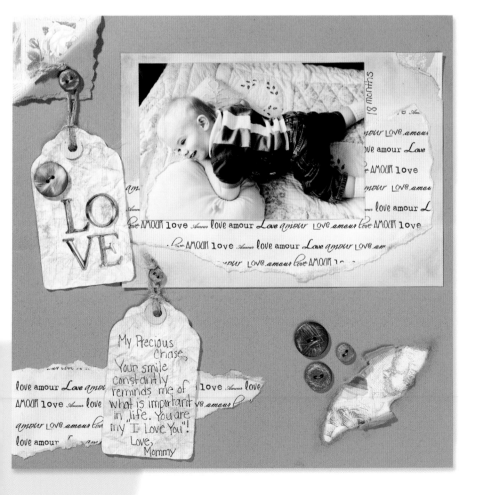

Love

Amy was inspired by a photographed quilt to create a soft, distressed look for her layout. Fold over upper left corner of brown cardstock; tear and chalk edges before slipping a scrap of patterned paper under folded edge. Attach button. Tear hole near bottom of brown cardstock; roll torn edges. Mount patterned paper behind torn window. Print loving words on ivory cardstock; tear two strips and chalk. Layer photo over torn printed strip on peach cardstock; tear and chalk corner. Mount patterned paper behind torn corner. Attach buttons on photo mat and page. Mount torn printed strip. Cut tags from distressed and chalked ivory cardstock; punch holes in circles punched from tan cardstock. Adhere letter stickers, mount button and journal. Tie with hemp string and hang from buttons.

Amy Warren, Tyler, Texas

Supplies: Letter stickers/(source unknown); tag template/Provo Craft; brown, ivory, tan and peach cardstocks; wire; hemp string; buttons; chalk

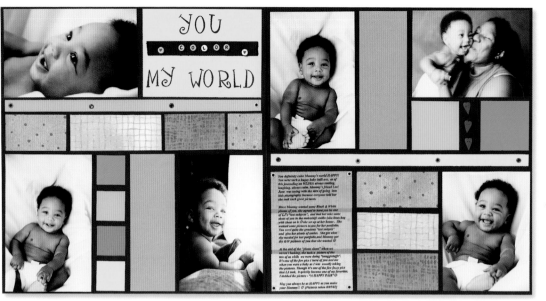

You Color My World

Natalie celebrates her son's vibrant personality with a striking color-blocked layout. Cut and punch solid and patterned papers to fit predetermined sections; mount with photos on black cardstock. Attach colored eyelets on strips. Stamp words for title; mount letter beads on black cardstock strip. Journal on vellum; attach with eyelets. Adhere heart buttons.

Natalie Cooper, Elkton, Maryland
Photos: Lori Jean Kopco, Bowie, Maryland

Supplies; Patterned paper/Provo Craft; letter beads/Darice; buttons/Making Memories; black cardstock and colored cardstocks; vellum; square punch; eyelets; heart

COLORS AND BLACK-AND-WHITE PHOTOS

Working with black-and-white photos opens up your options when selecting colors to use for backgrounds, mats and embellishments on your scrapbook spreads. When doing so, keep the following concepts in mind.

- Select colors that support and convey the mood of the picture, the event and your journaling. A celebratory activity is less likely to look joyful if your black-and-white photos are mounted on a largely gray page, for example. And if you are scrapbooking a photo of a napping child, you will conjure the peaceful quiet of the moment more easily if you mat or mount the photo in gentle pastels rather than riotous primary shades.

- Consider using colors based on the theme of your page. For example, a Christmas spread utilizing black-and-white photos might call for traditional Christmas colors of reds, greens and golds.

- Some black-and-white or sepia photos actually acquire undertones including pink, green and brown when processed. When selecting colors to use with your photos, take these undertones into consideration. Counter those undertones which you don't like by selecting contrasting papers. Accentuate the undertones which you like by surrounding them with similar colors.

- Using too many colors on pages featuring black-and-white photos can overwhelm the pictures. It is safest to select papers and embellishments in monochromatic tones.

- Black-and-white photos tend to take on the color tone of the paper on which it is immediately mounted. If you do not want this effect it is best to mat your photo in a neutral shade such as beige, black or white. Mat it again on the more vibrant color of your choice.

Supplies: Patterned paper, number and word tags/KI Memories; letter stickers/Creative Imaginations/Doodlebug Design; printed letter tiles/Scrapworks; square brads/Making Memories; antique brads/Karen Foster Design; square conchos/Scrapworks; black cardstock

Teething Time

Keisha lightens up the memory of her daughter's teething discomfort with a splash of color. Mount strips of black and white, striped and green patterned papers on black cardstock background. Print word on cardstock; layer with number tag and attach square brads. Highlight number 6 with yellow pen. Mount square conchos over printed letter tiles on cardstock strip; ink edges. Layer with photo and mount brads. Adhere title letter stickers. Attach square brad at end of black and white strip over word tag.

Keisha Campbell, Great Lakes, Illinois

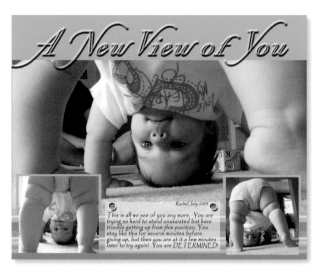

A New View of You

Jill can't figure out whether her daughter is content standing on her head or she simply stuck upside down. Re-create this computer-generated layout by mounting green cardstock border at top of enlarged photo. Handcut title from blue cardstock. Journal on vellum; mount with silver conchos layered over green jewels. Mat small photos on green cardstock; layer with striped patterned paper over bottom of enlarged photo.

Jill Caren, Matawan, New Jersey

Supplies: Green and blue cardstocks; vellum; silver conchos; green jewels

Baby

Keisha uses cheerful colors to capture the essence of her daughter's effortless smile. Layer patterned paper strips on black background cardstock. Enhance black-and-white photo using photo-editing software. Adhere flower sticker on striped tag. Layer word tag over printed definition. Affix title letter stickers. Mount faux wax seal with word tag at end of patterned paper strip; attach flower brad.

Keisha Campbell, Great Lakes, Illinois

Supplies: Patterned papers, word tags, patterned tag/KI Memories; letter stickers/ Deluxe Designs/Wordsworth; definition/Making Memories; flower sticker/Paper House Productions; flower brad/Jest Charming; faux wax seal/Creative Imaginations; black cardstock

Ray of Son-Shine

Brandy's selection of colors reflects her son's joyous personality. Layer border at left side of green patterned paper background with strips of blue and patterned paper. Adhere title letter stickers on blue strip. Print journaling on vellum; mount on page with brads. Double mat photo on solid and patterned papers; roughen and ink edges of second mat. Mount over circle punched from patterned paper and blue paper strip. Dangle star charm in window of preprinted slide frame; mount frame over blue paper and secure star with foam spacers. Layer patterned paper scraps on frame.

Brandy Logan, Hendersonville, North Carolina

Supplies: Patterned paper, preprinted slide frame/KI Memories; letter stickers/Creative Imaginations/Colorbök; metal star charm/Making Memories; blue cardstock; vellum; brads; chalk; fiber

Including Memorabilia on Your Pages

From hospital bracelets to first locks of hair, newbie outfits and booties, babies come with a lot of pint-sized accoutrements. Discover creative ways to encapsulate and include these precious mementos on your scrapbook spreads (pages 94-97), to be admired again and again.

Now I Lay Me Down to Sleep

Jennifer swaddles a favorite page with layers of tulle fabric. Roughen edges of blue paper; mat on ivory cardstock. Slip photo into preprinted frame on an angle; layer over preprinted bow. Mount baby's pillowcase. Wrap tulle across page, and secure. Layer walnut ink-stained tag with ephemera; attach small preprinted tags with swirl clip. Mount faux seal, watch face and parts; tie with ribbon. Print descriptive word on ivory cardstock; mount behind bookplate. Mount embellished tag, plastic memorabilia envelope, buttons and bookplate on fabric-wrapped page; slip hat inside plastic envelope.

Jennifer Bertsch, Tallahassee, Florida

Supplies: Frame, bow/My Mind's Eye; silver bookplate/Magic Scraps; tags/EK Success; faux wax seal/Creative Imaginations; ephemera/Foofala; blue and ivory cardstocks; tulle; swirl clip; watch face and parts; buttons; ribbon; plastic memorabilia envelope

First Haircut

Elsa illustrates how her son's first haircut transformed him from a baby to a young toddler. Single and double mat photos on colored cardstock; mount on patterned background paper. Tie fibers around double-matted photo. Mount matted square-punched photo with memorabilia envelope on cardstock; enclose lock of hair. Handcut printed title from green cardstock. Journal on vellum; attach to page with brads.

Elsa Duff, Whitecourt, Alberta, Canada

Supplies: Patterned paper/Paper Adventures; mulberry spring roll/Pulsar; sage cardstock; fiber; brads; memorabilia envelope

Charmed

Candi preserves the tiny bracelet that once fit her baby girl. Cut a large piece of patterned vellum; mount at right side of cream speckled cardstock background. Print journaling on patterned paper; crop and mount. Wrap rickrack across patterned paper; secure. Mount photos and plastic memorabilia envelope; insert bracelet in envelope. Adhere title letter stickers. String heart beads on wire; wrap around brads attached to page. Stamp date.

Candi Gershon, Fishers, Indiana

Supplies: Patterned paper and vellum/EK Success; letter stickers/Wordsworth; heart beads/Precious Accents; date stamp/Making Memories; cream speckled cardstock; memorabilia pocket; brads; wire; rickrack

Your First Outfit

Heather documented her son's first outfit without adding bulk to her layout. Scan clothing; print on photo paper and silhouette cut. Layer on blue cardstock background with photos. Journal on vellum; mount over photos with eyelets.

Heather Hornback, Sergeant Bluff, Iowa

Supplies: Eyelets; blue cardstock; vellum

Supplies: Embroidered tags/Me & My Big Ideas; embossed metal tag/K & Co.; heart buttons/Jesse James; blue cardstock; beads; buttons; safety pins; charms; embroidery floss; ribbon

I Am Richly Blessed

Nothing says "baby" quite like a cuddly terry cloth sleeper, or photo frames and an embellished quilt pieced together from soft baby sleepers. Stitch border just inside blue matted cardstock background; stitch buttons at corners. Print title, text and birth information on blue cardstock. Sew squares cut from baby sleepers together; stitch buttons. Stitch beaded segments around metal embossed tag. String bead strands across printed and stitched cardstock. Secure embroidered tags with safety pins. Hang cross and silver heart from safety pins. Wrap cardstock frame with terry cloth; string beads and attach safety pins at adjacent corners. Mount over cropped photo. Stitch printed cardstock; secure under beaded strands stitched across corners of square. Mount embroidered tags; stitch heart button. Mount embellished terry cloth quilt. Wrap ribbon across page and edges of quilt; secure. Frame photos with terry cloth fabric; wrap and secure fabric over photo edges. Tie corners of large frame with fibers; embellish with safety pins, beaded strand and stitched heart button. Wrap adjacent corners of small frame with beaded strands; secure safety pins. Stitch ivory heart button over torn cardstock heart. Stitch title cardstock; string beads across strip.

Andrea Lyn Vetten-Marley, Aurora, Colorado

Supplies: Distressed papers/Rusty Pickle; patterned paper/7 Gypsies; canvas for inkjet printers (source unknown); letter stamps/Ma Vinci's Reliquary/PSX Design; metal flower (source unknown); yellow cardstock; twill tape; fabric scraps; safety pins

First Favorite Books

Jeniece adds texture to the visual list of her daughter's favorite books with fabric and scanned book covers printed on canvas. Stamp title on distressed yellow paper; mount next to patterned paper on pink distressed background paper. Stitch together fabric squares and mount on page. Mat photo on pink tinted canvas; attach to fabric squares with safety pins. Mount metal flower. Scan book covers and print on canvas; silhouette and layer along bottom of page. Cover title and patterned paper seams with twill tape; attach safety pin. Stamp words and shapes on twill tape and photo.

Jeniece Higgins, Lake Forest, Illinois

Brennen's First Food

Christine incorporates real product labels from her son's first foods as a colorful border. Mount baby food label border along top and bottom of white cardstock background. Journal on white cardstock. Double mat journaling and photos on solid and patterned papers.

Christine Ramsey, Rockford, Illinois

Supplies: Patterned paper/Keeping Memories Alive; white cardstock; food labels

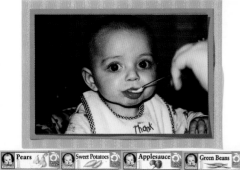

Supplies: Patterned paper/Chatterbox/Daisy D's; letter stickers/Creative Imaginations; foot stamp/Stamp Craft; safety pins/Making Memories; quilt pattern/Georgia Bonesteel; lace; fabric; embroidery floss; fibers; metal frame; eyelets; bookplate; kitchen accessories; crocheted flowers; beads

The Perfect Recipe for Love

Andrea cooks up a clever theme for a her daughter's birth announcement with a recipe card that lists the ingredients to a treasured recipe. Cut and layer patterned paper pieces for background using quilt pattern; stitch together. Border page with layered fibers. Wrap lace over adjacent corners; attach safety pins. Print title and text on patterned paper; stitch "recipe card" to page. Adhere letter stickers; embellish with miniature kitchen utensils, stamped footprints and crocheted flower. Mount title words on blue patterned paper behind bookplate tied with fibers. String heart charms on fiber; string through attached eyelets. Frame photo with quilted fabric; fold and secure fabric over sides of photo. Stitch along top; string beads on embroidery floss. Cross-stitch beaded design along bottom of fabric frame. Embellish corners with fiber bows, safety pins, heart charm and crocheted flower. Mount cropped photo behind metal frame.

Andrea Lyn Vetten-Marley, Aurora, Colorado

Supplies: Patterned paper, clear slide holder/Creative Imaginations; transparency/3M; letter stamps/Postmodern Design; blue cardstock; ribbon; staples; safety pins

Loved to Pieces

Old and new photos of a well-loved blanket enable Diana to document her daughter's most valuable possession. Mount patterned paper on blue cardstock background. Journal on transparency; layer over color photo. Staple corners and attach blanket yarns with safety pin. Stamp title and mount black-and-white photo on transparency. Print date on photo; crop to fit behind clear slide holder. Wrap ribbon around sides of slide holder; secure with safety pins and wrap across page.

Diana Hudson, Bakersfield, California

Kyle's Not So Happy Birthday

Michelle saves memorabilia from her son's birthday with a dimensionally layered image cut from paper birthday hats. Freehand cut large balloons from colored cardstock; layer on page with double matted photo. Tie embroidery floss to one balloon. Stamp title words on lavender cardstock and background. Punch letters into scalloped squares. Mount brads across top of page. Cut designs from birthday hats; layer designs over small freehand cut and shaded balloons with foam spacers. Cut title words from colored cardstock; outline letters with watermarker. Journal on vellum; mount brads at corners. Secure swirl clips at top and bottom of page.

Michelle Pendleton, Colorado Springs, Colorado

Supplies: Letter stamps/Hero Arts; lettering template/Frances Meyer; colored swirl clips, colored brads/Creative Impressions; watermarker/Tsukineko; red, yellow, pink, lavender and blue cardstocks; vellum; chalk; colored pencils; scalloped square punch; embroidery floss; brad

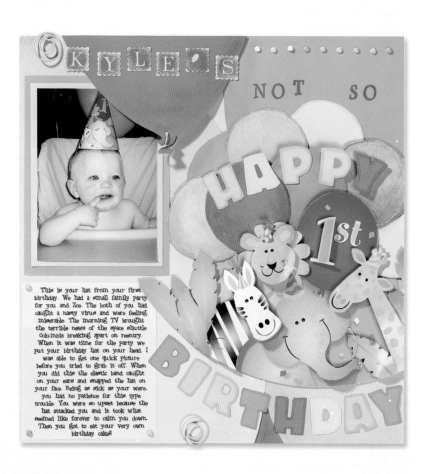

Ten Little Toes

Torrey cuts a dimensional window into a foam core background for treasured memorabilia. Cut window in foam core. Mount patterned paper on foam core; slice out window. Mount blue cardstock behind window with memorabilia. String letter beads on large safety pin. Adhere title, name and caption letter stickers; coat with crystal lacquer. Journal on transparency; stitch on decoratively trimmed patterned paper. Feed fabric strips through buckle; wrap around edges of page and secure. Attach conchos over buttons; add to title, journaling and fabric strips. Mount feet eyelets.

Torrey Miller, Thornton, Colorado
Photo: Stacy Moore, Boulder, Colorado

Supplies: Patterned paper, letter stickers/K & Co.; letter beads/Westrim; feet eyelets/Scraparts; conchos/Scrapworks; blue cardstocks; transparency; gingham fabric; buckle; foam core; safety pin; memorabilia; buttons; crystal lacquer

Joshua

Marianne contrasts a burst of vibrant color with the clean lines of a color-blocked layout. Mount enlarged photo on white glittered cardstock matted on black cardstock; attach brads. Cut black cardstock sections to size. Mount heart button on white cardstock; attach brads. Attach metal letter eyelets over white mesh. Attach square brads. Adhere word sticker labels; embellish with brads. Snip circles from top of letter charms; mount on black cardstock. Journal on white cardstock; layer over mesh on black cardstock. Attach eyelets and secure heart buttons.

Marianne Dobbs, Alpena, Michigan

Supplies: Glittered cardstock, metal number eyelets, metal letter charms/Making Memories; word sticker labels/Stampendous; layout template/Deluxe Designs; black and white cardstocks; black wire; silver brads; heart buttons; mesh

Supplies: Rub-on word/Making Memories; metal bookplate/Magic Scraps; white and black cardstocks; black eyelets

I Can Only Imagine

Rebecca assembles a list of personal thoughts, hopes and dreams for her baby's future. Print part of title, date and list on white cardstock. Layer list strips over part of matted photo on black cardstock; attach eyelets. Mat three cropped photos on one strip of white cardstock. Mount metal bookplate over date with eyelets. Mount printed title words; rub on white word transfer.

Rebecca Smith, Medina, Tennessee

Supplies: Swirl clips/Making Memories; page pebbles/Michael's; black and white cardstocks; printed vellum

Child of My Child

Wendy eloquently records the wonder of the world in her grandson's eyes. Mount enlarged photo on black cardstock background. Mat small photos on white cardstock strip; layer under printed vellum. Mount glass pebbles over specific poem words; attach swirl clips.

Wendy Bickford, Antelope, California

Mirror, Mirror

Jill captures her daughter's playful reflection with a familiar fairy tale title. Re-create this computer-generated page by cropping an enlarged photo into a curved shape; double mat. Print date on gold cardstock and part of title on black cardstock. Mount gold cardstock strips on black cardstock background. Layer gold and black letter stickers along photo's edge for a shadowed effect.

Jill Caren, Matawan, New Jersey

Supplies: Gold and black cardstocks; letter stickers

Beyond Comparison

Joanna was inspired by the design of a print ad to create a layout that captures the expressions of her baby boy. Horizontally mount large piece of blue cardstock 3" from top of black cardstock background. Mount photos and buttons on page. Print title and journaling on white cardstock; mat on blue cardstock.

Joanna Bolick, Black Mountain, North Carolina

Supplies: Blue, black and white cardstocks; buttons

A Kiss Could Never Be So Sweet

Love comes easy for Janice's daughter when she meets her new baby brother for the first time. Re-create this striking layout using only black and white cardstocks. Assemble phrase from large handcut letters and words printed on pieces of white and black cardstock. Cut black cardstock with text at bottom into strip; layer over white cardstock background, making sure to line up words. Print "kiss" on both black and white cardstocks; silhouette cut. Loosely adhere letters on cutting board with removable adhesive; horizontally slice both sets of letters using a ruler and craft knife. Mount top half of black letters over white letters; set aside. Cut black cardstocks with text at top into same size; mat on white cardstock. Silhouette cut image from black-and-white photo; layer on black cardstock and mat. Layer stair-stepped matted photo and text on background. Mount two-tone handcut word, making sure to line up color break with top of matted cardstock.

Janice Dye-Szucs, Oshawa, Ontario, Canada

Supplies: Black and white cardstocks

So Dayton

Mellette's son doesn't need a whole lot of "things" around him to bring out his humorous antics. Slice a 5¾" piece of patterned paper and a 5" piece of orange cardstock; mount next to each other on brown cardstock background. Create stitched accents by piercing holes. Lace paper yarn through holes; secure on back. Mount a strip of tan cardstock at bottom of page. Print title on orange cardstock; silhouette cut. Mount with silver letter tiles for title. Crop photos and mount.

Mellette Berezoski, Crosby, Texas

Supplies: Patterned paper/Karen Foster Design; silver letter tiles, paper yarn/Making Memories; orange, brown and tan cardstocks

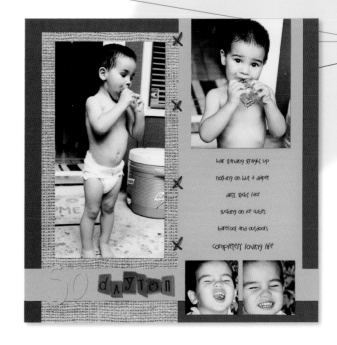

Funny Face

Holly shows why her baby never fails to put a smile on her face. Print journaling and poem on cream cardstock; mount with enlarged photo on brown cardstock background. Print title on cream cardstock; silhouette cut. Mount ribbon trim; wrap around edges and secure at back of page.

Holly VanDyne, Mansfield, Ohio

Supplies: Cream and brown cardstocks; ribbon

Learn Laughter

Bethany uses the colors of her son's stuffed Pooh Bear to re-create the joyful feeling her son has for his favorite character. Print quote on vellum and photo caption on gold cardstock. Ink edges of photo caption and tear edges of vellum. Stamp and write specific words on gold cardstock; ink edges and mount amongst quote and photo caption text. Layer together over photo on suede paper. Mount small matted photo over red paper yarn. Stitch corners of suede paper to red cardstock background with embroidery floss.

Bethany Fields, Amarillo, Texas
Photo: René Brown, Adrian, Texas
Poem: Wilferd A. Peterson

Supplies: Suede paper/Paper Adventures; letter stamps/Hero Arts; paper yarn/Making Memories; gold and red cardstocks; vellum; embroidery floss; ink

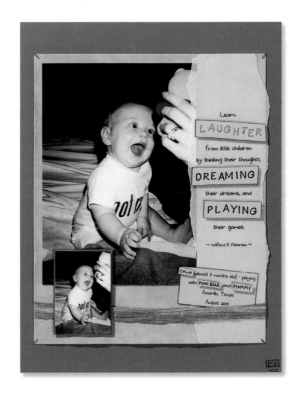

Bonnets and Ruffles

Peggy pairs a charming childhood photo with feminine stitched accents and embroidered flowers. Mat photo on peach cardstock; mount with metal corners on layered monochromatic background. Print title on patterned paper; cut freeform shape and mat. Cross-stitch to page with embroidery floss. Slice windows in orange cardstock strip; layer over lace trim embellished with embroidered flowers and heart beads. Mount metal frame over printed vellum. Border with orange fibers and attach metal corners. Stamp date.

Peggy Roarty, Council Bluffs, Iowa
Poem: Author unknown

Supplies: Patterned paper/PSX Design; date stamp, metal frame; metal photo corners/(Making Memories); peach and orange cardstocks: printed vellum/(source unknown); ivory lace trim; orange fibers; orange embroidery floss; heart beads

Supplies: Patterned papers/Anna Griffin; textured cardstock/(source unknown); letter sticker/Wordsworth; black tie clasp envelope; charm/(source unknown); black and white cardstocks

Name and a Blessing

Mindy secures the details of her daughter's blessing inside an elegant embellished black envelope. Mount patterned paper strip at left side of black cardstock background. Span enlarged photo across both pages; slice and mount at inside edges of both pages. Cut and layer textured cardstock next to enlarged photo and along bottom of pages. Mat smaller photo on patterned paper; machine stitch along top and bottom edges. Layer over textured cardstock and black tie clasp envelope. Adhere letter sticker on charm; attach to envelope string and secure. Cut small title words from patterned paper; handcut large title word from white cardstock.

Mindy Bush, Idaho Falls, Idaho

Imagine the Possibilities

The image of a newborn baby always makes Vicki think of the exciting possibilities that lie ahead. Layer cardstock strip over patterned paper; wrap decorative trim around page over paper seam. Mount vintage buttons; attach bookplate over stamped date with brads. Journal on vellum; stitch. Double mat photo; adhere with photo corners. Attach eyelets at bottom of second mat; string sheer ribbon through eyelets and tie in a bow.

Vicki Harvey, Champlin, Minnesota

Supplies: Patterned paper/Anna Griffin; date stamp/Office Depot; label holder/Anima Designs; pink cardstock; vellum; eyelets; photo corners; ribbon; decorative trim; metal bookplate; buttons; ink

Beautiful Girl

April incorporates a collaged CD on her layout alongside the story of a special daddy-daughter musical ritual. Layer patterned papers for background; mount mesh ribbon across page. Crumple, flatten, ink and stain ivory cardstock. Stain tan cardstock with diluted walnut-ink. Collage CD with patterned papers; emboss edges with bronze ink and embossing powder. Mount metal bookplate over printed name; tie small tag. Tie fibers and sheer ribbon on CD; attach safety pin. Mat black cardstock on walnut ink-stained tan cardstock; tear bottom edges of both cardstocks. Layer photo with black cardstock corners over distressed ivory cardstock; mount with CD on layered, torn and stained cardstock strips. Wrap fibers and tie; secure ends with brads. Tie decorative button with embroidery floss; hang small tags tinted with walnut ink. Print title and journaling on vellum; double mat with distressed and black cardstocks. Mount brads and decorative heart; wrap mesh ribbon around journaling strip.

April Kleinfeldt, Kernersville, North Carolina

Supplies; Patterned paper/7 Gypsies/Anna Griffin/Frances Meyer/Penny Black; mini tags/American Tag; ivory, black and tan cardstocks; vellum; mesh ribbon; fibers; sheer gold ribbon; metal bookplate; brass brads; CD; safety pin; walnut ink

Curls

Misty's daughter encountered a sticky gum situation and had to have a few of her curls cut off. Layer purple metallic mesh over torn beige cardstock; mount on plum cardstock background. Adhere fibers along sides of angled photo. Mount gathered tulle on twisted lavender spring roll. Secure swirl clips over edges of cardstock. Place lock of hair in keepsake envelope. Mount paper flowers.

Misty Posey, Decatur, Alabama
Photo: Carol Hutto, Courtland, Alabama

Supplies: Lavender spring roll/Pulsar; metallic purple mesh/Jest Charming; swirl clips/Making Memories; paper flowers/Robin's Nest; beige and plum cardstock; silver fibers; lavender tulle; plastic keepsake envelope

Supplies: Patterned papers/KI Memories; rub-on word/Making Memories; black ink; extra thick embossing powder; watermark ink

Perfection

Jennifer adds a unique perspective to an angled photo of her son with inked patterned paper strips. Slice varied sizes of strips of monochromatic patterned papers brushed with black ink. Layer as horizontal design on patterned paper background; ink edges. Rub on black word transfer for title. Mount photo on angle. Add random texture by pressing watermark pad on areas of background; sprinkle with extra thick embossing powder and heat emboss.

Jennifer Kotas, Poughkeepsie, New York

Supplies: Ivory letter tiles/Westrim Crafts; heart buttons/Jesse James; ivory and blue cardstocks; sheer embroidered fabric; satin cord

When My Baby Smiles at Me

Sarah uses the words of an old jazz song to journal her feelings when her son smiles. Cover two-thirds of ivory cardstock background with sheer embroidered fabric. Print title and song lyrics on blue cardstock; tear vertical edges. Mount ivory letter tiles as part of title. Print photo caption on ivory cardstock. String heart buttons on satin cord; wrap around double-matted photo and along top and bottom of page.

Sarah Devendorf, Nashville, Tennessee
Lyrics: Ted Lewis Orchestra

FIVE

LOVING *Ian*

To my son whose eyes so bright,
look at the world with brand new sight.
Whether I hold you close to me,
or you stand embraced around my knee,
my heart speaks words so beautifully clear,
I will love you always, my boy, so dear.

— Susan Schiltz

joy

JUL 1 4 2003

MOMMY
& IAN
· 9 MOS.

The Supporting Cast

From the moment you first lay eyes on your newborn and your heart turned somersaults in your chest, you were completely and utterly his. No matter how much you may have longed to hold on to adult sanity, you found yourself pulling ridiculously comical faces in outlandish attempts to get your child to smile—uttering nonsense babbles in a search of a common language. Were there not an obvious reason for your antics, you might have been carted off to someplace padded. However, anyone who has ever had a baby in her life—a parent, an aunt or uncle, cousin, friend or grandparent, has found herself in the same situation and so society, as a whole, understands and makes exceptions for these otherwise bizarre behaviors. You just can't help being a fan when there is a baby around. Showcase those special photos of your baby with his most adoring supporters on pages that ring with praise and love.

I don't know why they say "You have a baby." The baby has you.
Gallagher

Dreaming

Carrie celebrates the moment she realized that her dreams had come true on a partially hidden tag that pulls out to reveal her journaled thoughts. Tear and chalk edges of photos; layer on patterned background paper. Add focus to elements in photos with plastic glass squares mounted with spray adhesive. Print title on ivory cardstock; tear and chalk edges. Adhere letter stickers over small walnut-stained and chalked tag tied with twine. Journal on walnut-stained paper; tear and layer on walnut-stained tag tied with twine. Slip behind enlarged photo.

Carrie O'Donnell, Newburyport, Massachusetts

Supplies: Patterned paper/Karen Foster Design; letter stickers/Creative Imaginations/EK Success; small walnut-inked tag/7 Gypsies; large walnut-inked tag/www.absolutely everything.com; ivory cardstock; walnut-stained paper; twine; plastic glass squares; chalk

Special Pooh Song

Stacy re-creates the soft, worn feeling of a favorite quilt with distressed papers, stitched accents and lyrics to a beautiful bedtime song. Crumple, flatten, sand and chalk yellow and blue patterned papers. Stitch yellow patterned paper onto yellow cardstock background; ink edges. Layer photos over pieces of distressed blue patterned paper stitched to background. Journal on blue patterned paper; tear small pieces from edges and chalk. Mat on yellow patterned cardstock with inked edges. Print song lyrics on yellow patterned paper; slice into strips and ink edges. Slice border strip and tear corner from brown cardstock; tear small pieces from edge of border strip. Mount letter tiles, tinted letter stickers and letter pebbles for title. Adhere Pooh stickers. Sew cross stitches with brown embroidery floss on lyric strips, journaling, border strip and along stitched edges of patterned paper.

Stacy McFadden, Victoria, Australia
Lyrics: Kenny Loggins

Supplies: Patterned paper/Mustard Moon; letter stickers/(source unknown); letter pebbles/Making Memories; letter tiles/(source unknown); Pooh stickers/(source unknown); yellow and brown

Supplies: Patterned papers/7 Gypsies/Karen Foster Design/SEI; letter stamps/PSX Design; patterned vellum/Colorbök; white and tan cardstocks; metal-rimmed tag/Creative Imaginations; clip

Love Beyond Measure

Hidden letters layered near measuring tape strips speak to Joanna's immeasurable love for her family. Print title and heart on white cardstock; add patterned paper strip across heart. Mount photo over a large piece of patterned vellum layered over same size yellow cardstock. Slice and remove paper from inside of metal rim tag. Mount metal frame over cropped photo; apply adhesive along back sides and bottom of photo tag, leaving the top and center available for notes to slip behind. Cut measuring tape strips from patterned paper; mount across page. Mount additional tape strip section under edge of photo. Roughen area on strip; stamp words. Write love letters on back of tan paper; tear top edge and stamp names on front. Slip behind photo tag and attach to measuring tape strip with circle clip. Frame page with torn strips of navy cardstock.

Joanna Bolick, Black Mountain, North Carolina

My Love for You

Kim layers papers printed with letters, numbers and a measuring tape image as symbols of a mother's immeasurable love. Print title word near bottom of brown cardstock background. Layer and mount pieces of black, white and yellow patterned papers. Mat photo on yellow patterned paper. Transfer rub-on letters to brads; attach on page as title words. Adhere stickers on white patterned paper; cut around sticker lines.

Kim Haynes, Harrah, Oklahoma

Supplies: Patterned papers/7 Gypsies; letter stickers/Wordsworth; rub-on letters, brads/Creative Imaginations; brown cardstock; silver brads

Proud New Daddy

Bright, fresh colors represent the new life and new love in a man's life. Layer patterned paper over black cardstock strip sewed on yellow cardstock background. Mat photo on white cardstock; layer with walnut-stained tag tied with ribbon. Adhere letter stickers on tag for title. Mount metal bookplate over date stamped on white cardstock; tie ribbon and wrap across page. Mount flower brads on bookplate. Write sentiment.

Katherine Teague, New Westminster, British Columbia, Canada

Supplies: Patterned paper/7 Gypsies; letter stickers/Creative Imaginations/SEI; date stamp/(source unknown); walnut-stained tag/Rusty Pickle; black, white and yellow cardstocks; gingham ribbon; metal bookplate; flower brad

Supplies: White and black cardstocks; vellum; fibers; photo corners; swirl clips; black photo corners

A Year of Love

Wendy created clever fold-over cards that open to reveal photos and messages of love written to her grandson by close family members. Print an acronym title on white cardstock; mat on black cardstock. Create horizontal and vertical fold-over cards from scored and folded black cardstock. Mount black-and-white photo on outside of card with black photo corners. Open card; mount color photo and personal handwritten message. Print photo captions on vellum; mount next to each photo card. Tie fibers to swirl clips; add as an embellishment and secure on photo card flap as the "lift." Twist fibers; secure with swirl clips across top and bottom of page.

Wendy Bickford, Antelope, California

Leah Abigail Powell

Bernie frames a beautiful sepia-toned portrait with torn, monochromatic patterned papers and vellums. Tear patterned paper and vellum; layer on white cardstock background. Print quote on patterned paper; tear around words and mount over right side of enlarged photo matted on white cardstock. Tear and chalk edges of mat; wrap with lavender fibers and attach teddy bear charm. Journal on white cardstock; dab with watermark ink and chalk.

Bernie Silvan, Drexel Hill, Pennsylvania
Poem: www.twopeasinabucket.com

Supplies: Patterned paper/PSX Design; patterned vellum/Hot Off The Press; teddy bear charm/(source unknown); watermark ink/Tsukineko; white cardstock; purple chalk, fibers

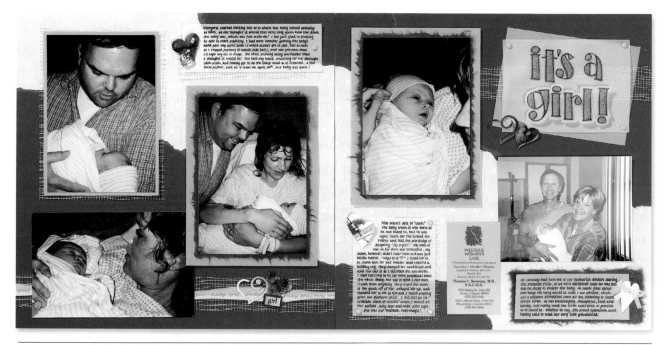

Supplies: Patterned paper/Keeping Memories Alive/Colors by Design; mesh/Magenta; stickers/All My Memories; ribbon; metal word eyelet, silver heart charms, pink snaps/Making Memories; metal hearts/Heartland Crafts; burgundy cardstock; vellum; mulberry paper; wire; microbeads; embossing powder; crystal lacquer

It's a Girl!

Embellished and embossed hearts accentuate Michelle's story about her daughter's entrance into the world. Tear varied pieces of burgundy cardstock; mount on patterned paper. Sand metal heart; press heart on watermark pad and sprinkle with embossing powders; heat set. Write "It's a" title words on vellum; color inside of letters. Write "girl" on a second piece of vellum; silhouette cut and mount on title block with foam spacers. Adhere microbeads to insides of letters with crystal lacquer. Cut two narrow strips of mesh; layer one strip at top of right page in between vellum title and patterned paper. Attach pink snaps at corners of title block; secure one snap over decorative heart charm layered with embossed heart. Adhere sticker strip over mesh strip at bottom of left page. Embellish with decorative heart charm, pink snap, embossed heart and silver word eyelet mounted on burgundy cardstock. Double mat three photos on patterned and torn mulberry paper or mesh; mount memorabilia and all photos on page. Journal on vellum. Attach journaling block over mesh with snaps at bottom of right page. Embellish silver heart with torn mulberry paper and border sticker scrap; wrap with beaded wire. Embellish another silver heart with bow; mount over journaling matted on torn mulberry paper. Embellish journaling block at top of left page: mat on mesh. Mount embossed heart wrapped with beaded wire and silver heart charm at left of text.

Michelle Pesce, Arvada, Colorado
Photos: Joan Fox, Lafayette, California

Sept. 1961

Wanda showcases a vintage photo of herself as a baby with journaling about favorite childhood memories. Photocopy dictionary definition on laser-cut paper; tear edges and layer under enlarged photo on white cardstock background. Wrap mesh ribbon along left side of background cardstock; mount flowers. Print date for title on white cardstock and reversed-text journaling on vellum. Cut jagged edges around journaling and outline with gold paint pen; attach with gold brads.

Wanda Santiago-Cintron, Deerfield, Wisconsin

Supplies: Laser cut paper/Hot off The press; white cardstock; vellum; mesh; gold brads; flowers; gold paint pen

Daddy and Chase

The voice of a child speaks volumes in the poem Mary selected to accompany the photograph of her husband and son. Layer enlarged photo with torn patterned paper over blue cardstock background. Print poem and photo caption on vellum; tear edges and mount with small silver brads. Mount metal feet plaque.

Mary Hammerberg, Paw Paw, Michigan
Poem: www.twopeasinabucket.com

Supplies: Patterned paper/Karen Foster Design; metal feet plaque/Making Memories; blue cardstock; vellum; silver brads

Walk along beside me daddy, and
hold my little hand.

I have so many things to learn
that I don't understand.

Teach me things to keep me safe
from dangers everyday.

Show me how to do my best at
home and at play.

Every child needs a gentle hand to
guide them as they grow.

So walk along beside me, Daddy,
we have a long way to go.

Daddy and Chase
July, 2002
Lake Michigan

Supplies: Patterned paper, quote stickers, word stickers, dragonfly stickers/Colorbök; green paper; vellum; square punch; fibers; gold eyelets; skeleton leaves

Love Forever

Pam assembles a quick and easy page with word and quote stickers that express the effortless relationship between mother and daughter. Punch squares in border strip; wrap with fiber. Layer over vellum and mat on green paper; adhere dragonfly stickers. Mount succession of photos above border strip. Double mat one photo with layered patterned and solid paper; wrap fibers around first mat. Mount skeleton leaves. Adhere quote and word stickers on vellum; layer over photos. Attach large eyelets on left page.

Pam Easley, Bentonia, Mississippi

Daddy's Girl

Candi answers the inevitable question of family resemblance with a visual comparison of Mom's and Dad's baby photos. Mount patterned paper over brown cardstock for background. Print journaling on ivory cardstock; mount on brown border at bottom of page. Mount photos; adhere title stickers next to large photo and for captions under cropped photos. Wrap fibers around page under enlarged photo; secure. Adhere pewter heart sticker.

Candi Gershon, Fishers, Indiana

Supplies: Patterned paper/C-Thru Ruler; letter stickers/Creative Imaginations; pewter heart sticker/Magenta; brown and ivory cardstocks; fibers

You Are Our Joy

Wanda selects images of family and favorite toys to reflect the innocence that is the center of a baby's world. Layer blue vellum over enlarged photo mounted on tan cardstock for background; attach brads at vellum corners. Triple mat photo on colored cardstock. Journal on vellum; triple mat and attach brads. Layer title printed on vellum over photo border sticker; attach brads.

Wanda Santiago-Cintron, Deerfield, Wisconsin

Supplies: Photo sticker border/EK Success; tan cardstock; blue vellum; brads

Look

Shelley creates an eye-opening page with fabric and layered papers. Mount wide torn piece of patterned paper on right, and narrow torn patterned strip on left side of cranberry textured cardstock. Adhere stamped burlap scrap. Mount pieces of coordinated cardstock and vellum over burlap. Mount close-up picture embellished with cord and brads. Add journaling created by running vellum strips through label maker; mount one on buckled ribbon and the other on cardstock strip and adhere to page. Add photo to metal-rimmed tag and mount with letter stickers. Mount photo of baby with father on layered paper scraps and embellish with label holder. Create title with stencils and metallic rub-ons. Journal on transparency, wrap with fibers and mount.

Shelley Rankin, Fredericton, New Brunswick, Canada

Supplies: Patterned paper/Creative Imaginations; lettering templates/(source unknown); tag, pewter flower/Making Memories; burgundy cardstock; vellum; transparency; black cord, pink fibers, label-maker

My Little Man

Christine keeps her husband's "anti-cutesy" request in mind when selecting colors, textures and patterned papers for her "little man" layout. Print title and journaling on brown patterned cardstock. Tear a slim and a wide strip of blue patterned paper; mount at sides of background cardstock. Chalk tags; add color to crumpled and flattened white paper with green and red chalks. Layer preprinted images over torn and distressed paper, mount on tags and wrap with hemp string. Tie hemp to tags; mount on page with foam spacers. Mount preprinted image at bottom of page. Mat photos on brown cardstock. Attach gold snaps at top of page above photo.

Christine Drumheller, Zeeland, Michigan

Supplies: Patterned paper/Frances Meyer; preprinted images/EK Success; tags/DMD; gold snaps/ Making Memories; hemp; chalk

Daddy's Love

Carrie was inspired to declare her love by an intimate moment between her husband and son. Enhance photos with photo-editing software. Journal on tan cardstock. Mat small photos and journaling on brown cardstock; layer over matted patterned paper. Mount page pebble.

Carrie O'Donnell, Newburyport, Massachusetts

Supplies: Patterned paper/Penny Black; page pebble/Making Memories; tan and brown cardstocks

Priceless

A candid photo illustrating a mother's adoration needs only one word to describe it. Tear bottom edge of a strip of patterned paper; mount on black textured cardstock. Mount ribbon along edge of patterned paper. Adhere black title letter stickers on white cardstock; silhouette cut. Double mat photo on decoratively cut green cardstock and green vellum. Adhere quote on vellum; double mat on green and black cardstocks. Mount with foam spacers and attach swirl clip. Stamp date on metal-rimmed tag; tie with ribbon.

Ellen Hargrove, Jenks, Oklahoma
Photo: Melissa Hall of Lighthouse Studio, Lawton, Oklahoma

Supplies: Patterned paper/7 Gypsies; letter stickers/Creative Imaginations; quote/Daisy D's; black, white and green cardstocks; swirl clip; metal-rimmed tag; ribbon

A Son Brings a Father a Joy...

Rachel adds a masculine element to an endearing father/son layout with the look of faux metallic and neon letters and shapes. Recreate the shine and glow of metallic and neon elements with metallic paint or felt-tip pens, metallic pigment powder or metallic rub-ons and chalks shaded around shapes and letters. Frame page with thin strips of pastel colored cardstocks; mount assembled punched squares at corners. Print or color copy photos in single tones. Assemble title from letter stickers and handcut words in a variety of sizes. Freehand cut or punch large hearts from black cardstock; outline and shade with colored metallic medium of choice. Silhouette cut names printed on colored cardstock; mat on black cardstock and layer over hearts.

Rachel Dickson, Calgary, Alberta, Canada

Supplies: Pastel and black cardstocks; square and heart punches; letter stickers; metallic paint or felt-tip pens; metallic pigment powder or metallic rub-ons

My First Bath

Elsa captures the small stature of a newborn baby curled inside a plastic bowl for his first bath. Layer embossed cardstock over patterned vellum matted on white cardstock. Write title words on metal-rimmed tags; shade with chalk and attach with brads. Cut large title word from white cardstock; chalk. Journal on vellum; tear bottom edge and layer over mesh on white cardstock. Embellish page with clusters of colored buttons.

Elsa Duff, Whitecourt, Alberta, Canada

Supplies: Patterned vellum/It Takes Two; embossed cardstock/Canada Scrapbooks!; letter template/Scrap Pagerz; white cardstock; vellum; mesh; metal-rimmed tags; brads; buttons; chalk

The Alexander Family

Angelina's proud announcement shows how a baby turns a couple into a family. Triple mat large photo. Wrap third mat with yellow ribbon and tie; layer with dark blue cardstock. Adhere poem and letter stickers on white and blue cardstocks. Cut title word strip; attach brads. Mount poem with photo corners. Tie metal-rimmed tags to ribbon; adhere letter stickers on rectangle tag and journal on circle tag. Single mat photos on white cardstock.

Angelina Schwarz, New Castle, Pennsylvania

Supplies: Letter stickers/Creative Imaginations/Provo Craft; poem sticker/Frances Meyer; metal-rimmed circle, rectangle tags/Making Memories; dark blue, blue and white cardstocks; yellow ribbon; silver brads; tan photo corners

Soapy Siblings

Valerie uses bubbles cut from layers of quilt batting on a fresh layout that's good clean fun. Mat two photos on one piece of blue cardstock; double and triple mount on patterned paper and white cardstock. Adhere word sticker and mount on patterned cardstock background. Assemble letter title stickers on blue cardstock to curve around oval tag. Mat on white cardstock. Adhere remaining title letter stickers on metal-rimmed tag; add fibers and layer over blue title block. Journal on vellum; circle cut and mount with bubble stickers. Draw bathtub on ivory cardstock; cut out and chalk. Cut cotton material for towel and drape over bathtub; mount on page with foam spacers next to bath stickers. Rub descriptive word transfer on blue cardstock; adhere adhesive tiles and pre-made dimensional stickers. Create a collection of bubbles: mount small and large circles cut from thin layers of quilt batting along with page pebbles, vellum circles and bubble stickers.

Valerie Salmon, Carmel, Indiana

Supplies: Patterned paper/Colorbök/Sonburn; letter stickers/Creative Imaginations/Doodlebug Design/SEI; pre-made dimensional stickers/EK Success; blue and white cardstocks; metal-rimmed tag; page pebbles; square tiles; quilt batting

Beach Bum

Sam exposes the official words that a beach bum lives with a whimsical combination of fonts and sizes. Layer patterned and solid papers with torn and inked edges over blue background paper. Tear four pieces of blue patterned paper in graduating sizes. Layer at lower right corner of page; roll torn edges. Stamp words on library card and pocket; wrap with fibers and tuck among layered corner. Mount letter tiles for title. Affix sea glass wrapped with wire; feed wire ends through pierced holes, twist and secure. Stamp word on wire-wrapped microscope slide with multi-surface ink. Feed wire ends through pierced holes on photo; twist and secure.

Sam Cousins, Shelton, Connecticut

Supplies: Patterned papers/(source unknown); letter stamps/Hero Arts/PSX Design; silver letter tiles/Creative Imaginations; library card pocket/www.Scrapsahoy.com; library card pocket/www.Alteredpages.com; multi-surface ink/Tsukineko; microscope slide/www.Manofev.com; fibers; sea glass; wire

Cuddling With Grandma

Even at a young age, a baby knows there is nothing more dreamy than snuggling in your grandmother's arms. Print title on vellum and journaling on white cardstock. Tear vellum edges; layer over patterned paper with torn edges. Attach to matted patterned paper background with eyelets. Mat journaling; mount over cardstock strip. Silhouette cut dragonfly from patterned paper; mount on metal-rimmed tag.

Linda Beeson, Ventura, California

Supplies: Patterned paper/Creative Imaginations/Daisy D's; white cardstock; vellum; metal-rimmed tags; green eyelets

Journaling Ideas

A picture may be worth a thousand words, but well-chosen and well-delivered words can do something no picture can: add names, dates, details and perceptions to a spread. Good journaling can be funny, uplifting, emotionally moving and exceptionally creative. Integrating journaling on scrapbook pages is an art in itself. Here (pages 116-119) are some great journaling ideas that will get your writing muse inspired.

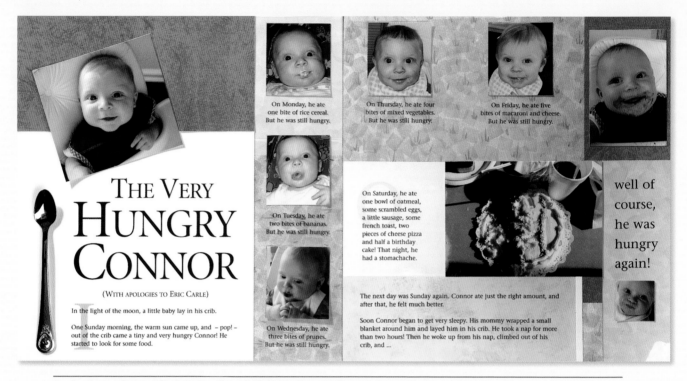

Supplies: Patterned papers/Okie Dokie Press/Provo Craft; blue, red, green, yellow and white cardstocks; transparency; spoon

The Very Hungry Connor

Susan adapts the theme and colorful appearance of a favorite children's book to a collection of photos illustrating her son's healthy appetite. Lightly draw lines for blocked design on white cardstock background. Cut blue, red, green and yellow patterned papers to fit blocked sections. Print title and story on transparency; print colored capital letters on white cardstock. Layer transparency with story lines over printed capital letters and on pages under photos. Mount spoon.

Susan Cyrus, Broken Arrow, Oklahoma

TITLE IDEAS FOR PAGES STARRING BABY

A great page title sets the mood for a spread and provides a headline that puts the art in perspective. Here are some great ideas for award-winning titles. Use them as they are or let them launch your own brainstorming session.

Leave 'em laughing in the aisles	Chick flick	Presenting, in person...
Love it, baby, love it!	Tear-jerker	Walk of Fame
Take one	Take a bow	Star treatment
Making the big time	On location	Roll 'em
Coming soon to a theatre near you!	Hammin' it up for the camera	You're a natural
Feature presentation	You oughta' be in pictures!	A silent picture
Quiet on the set!	A real showstopper	A perfect head shot
Action film	There's no business like show business	

CREATIVE QUOTES

Even strong writers can find themselves stuck for journaling sentiments. When that happens you may wish to reach for a book of famous quotations, or find them online. Here are a few examples of memorable insights murmured throughout the years.

The phrase "working mother" is redundant. - Jane Sellman

I don't know why they say "You have a baby." The baby has YOU. - Gallagher

Before I got married, I had six theories about bringing up children. Now I have six children and no theories. - John Wilmot

When I was born, I was so surprised I couldn't talk for a year and a half. - Gracie Allen

Father asked us what was God's noblest work. Anna said men, but I said babies. Men are often bad; babies never are. - Louisa May Alcott

No animal is so inexhaustible as an excited infant. - Amy Leslie

Invest in the future; have a child and teach her well. - Unknown

Little children are still the symbol of the eternal marriage between love and duty. - George Eliot Romola

We find delight in the beauty and happiness of children that makes the heart too big for the body. - Ralph Waldo Emerson

Children need love, especially when they do not deserve it. - Harold Hulbert

A baby is God's opinion that the world should go on. - Carl Sandburg

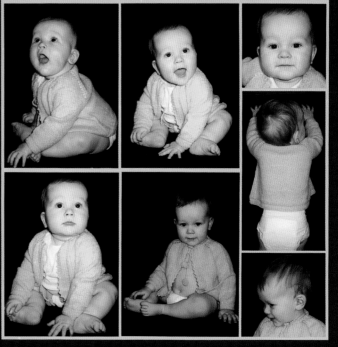

The Sweater

Nancy documents the lessons learned from a late great-grandmother and the gift of a handmade sweater. Crop photos to fit blocked layout; mount on matted yellow cardstock. Superimpose journaling over scanned sweater image with photo-editing software; print and silhouette cut. Mount on layers of black and yellow cardstocks.

Nancy Korf, Portland, Oregon

Supplies: Yellow and black cardstocks

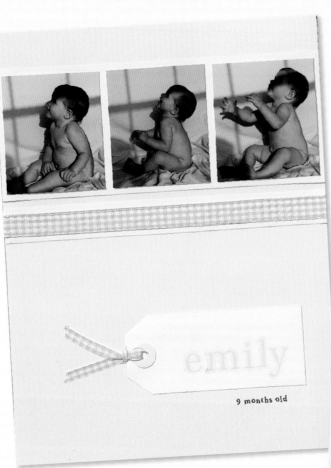

9 months old

- At 9 months old you are such an active little girl, exploring the world around you every minute. You are growing & learning & changing so much we can't hardly believe it.
- Your eyes are a mix between mom & dad's—they're grayish blue around the outside & brown in the middle
- weigh 19 pounds & are 28 inches tall
- Sleep with your teddy bear at night, on your side hugging him. Go to sleep so good.
- Always taking off your shoes, especially when we drive anywhere in the car
- If mom or dad say "I'm gonna get you" you squeal & turn & 'RUN' …at least you think you're running. You're really only walking.
- Into everything—Buddy's food, the garbage, the toilet…
- Switched from 2 naps a day to 1
- Your laugh is a high-pitched little scream! So funny!
- Understand "Do not touch."
- Everyone is so amazed at how well you get around for how little you are. At church you spend a lot more time in the hallways with mom & dad these days.
- Walk around the house carrying things in your mouth…toys, moms keys
- You say 'Mama' and 'Dada'

- Use your L.H. more than R.H.
- can wave Bub-bye
- started to blow kisses
- If we ask you "How big is Emily?" you put your little arms up in the air as we say "So Big!"
- Started clapping
- Favorite foods are bananas, cheerios, cantaloupe, pancakes, avocado (if mom mixes it with some fruit), fishy crackers, cheese cubes. Finger food! You aren't a very picky eater, you'll eat most things as long as you can do it by yourself.
- love swimming at the pool with mom & dad. You've been underwater & have fun in your little tube float.
- love other little kids. You just squeal & babble away when you see them
- aren't shy, you'll pretty much go to anyone
- You find it fun to empty cupboards & drawers.
- If you get into the bathroom you take all the shampoo & soaps from around the edge & throw them in the tub
- You're hair is long enough to put in a little pony tail right on top or pull back in a little brett (your little swoosh at the front that permanently parts to the right) We can't put them in too long before we go anywhere though or you pull them out

- putting your binky in mom & dad's mouth is a fun game. We'll hold the 'dry' end in our mouth & you laugh like it is the silliest thing! Then you'll grab it back
- need binky for naps & bedtime
- when you have your binky in you hold the bottom edge of it in side your mouth with your two little front teeth! It looks so funny!
- fascinated with teeth–you'll stick your finger in mom & dad's mouths to find ours
- have 2 little teeth of your own on the bottom, front & center
- You're walking! Still a little awkwardly but as many times as you fall down on your bum you just get right back up again & keep on moving! Very determined!
- Speaking of moving— you rarely S T O P
- Don't need a table or couch to pull up to standing anymore.
- fetish with paper, if we leave any lying around you'll snatch it up & EAT IT!
- Buddy's bone is a favorite toy, he'll chase you around trying to get it back, but you always put it in your mouth so we have to take it away! You know buddy's name, will look right at him when we ask "Where's Buddy?"
- Give mom & dad kisses (with your mouth wide open!!!)
- Easy-going, sociable, curious

Emily

Rebecca is able to keep the focus of her layout on photos of her daughter despite the large amount of text because of her choice of neutral colored elements and papers. Mount succession of three cropped photos on white cardstock strip. Stitch gingham ribbon on white cardstock strip. Cut tag from white cardstock; adhere letter stickers for title. Punch hole in cream punched circle and tie with gingham ribbon. Stamp age below tag. Print columns of text on white and cream textured cardstocks. Slice columns printed on cream cardstock into strips and layer. Horizontally and vertically slice cropped photos; reassemble photos at tops of columns.

Rebecca Cooper, Claresholm, Alberta, Canada

Supplies: Cream textured cardstock/(source unknown); letter stickers/SEI; white cardstock; gingham ribbon; circle punch

BC (before Connor), AD (after delivery)

Nancy compares life before and after the arrival of her son with a humorous and descriptive list. Print title, list and dates on white cardstock. Cut dates and list into angled shapes; rub edges with colored ink pads. Stamp decorative squares on white cardstock title blocks; mount acrylic letters. Journal around edges and mat on colored cardstock. Mat photos on colored cardstock; secure dates with square paper clip.

Nancy Korf, Portland, Oregon

Supplies: Acrylic letters/Heidi Grace Designs; date stamp, square paper clips/Making Memories; decorative square stamps/Stampin' Up!; white and colored cardstocks; colored inks

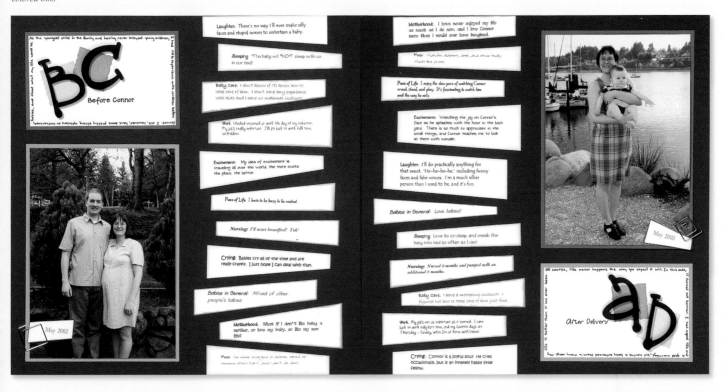

JOURNALING ABOUT BABY

Some say that pictures speak louder than words; however, those who feel comfortable laying their thoughts and feelings down in ink know how invaluable carefully selected words can be. Take the time to journal about your baby and ask those you love to share their thoughts as well.

- Write a pre-birth letter to your baby detailing your feelings about the upcoming birth. Include thoughts about any fears you might have and your dreams for your baby's future.

- Record the process of selecting your child's name. How did you go about making the selection? What were your least favorite names? What names made your short list? How did you narrow them down, and what were the deciding factors?

- Journal about your child's birth. How did you know you were in labor? What was the trip to the hospital like? What did you discuss with your baby's father while you awaited the birth? What did you use as a focal point during labor?

- What was the first thing that popped into your head when you saw your newborn baby for the first time?

- What did others say when they saw your baby for the first time? How did they act?

- Ask those you are close to write a note welcoming your baby to the world. Have them mention those joys and blessings they would gift to your child.

- Song lyrics and poems can offer powerful messages that touch your heart. Write down the lyrics or words of your favorites and journal about why they are meaningful to you.

- Record details such as the exact time your baby was born. Where? Who was in the room? How long was the labor?

- Record fun information including which songs were most popular at the time your baby was born, what shows were hits on Broadway, what novels were on the best seller lists, what fashions were being touted, what technology was just being introduced, what new model cars were being released.

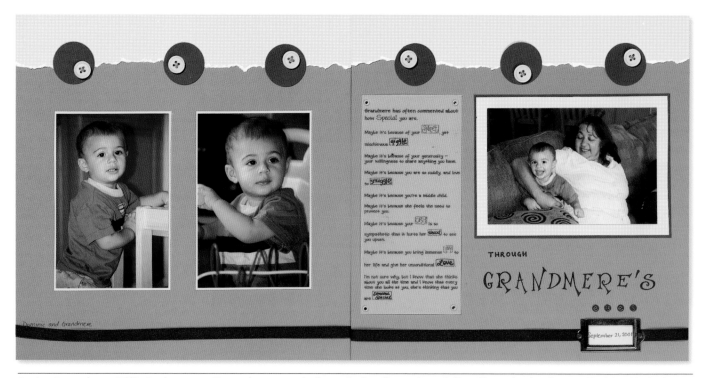

Supplies: Patterned paper/Pebbles Inc.; letter stamps/Stampendous; green and yellow cardstocks; vellum; circle punch; blue ribbon; embroidery floss; metal bookplate; blue brads; yellow eyelets; yellow buttons

Through Grandmere's Eyes

Inspired by the design of a print ad, Michelle lists her son's lovable qualities using a variety of fonts to emphasize descriptive words. Stitch buttons on punched circles with embroidery floss; layer on torn patterned paper border mounted on green cardstock. Single and double mat photos on patterned paper and solid cardstock. Print list on vellum in a variety of fonts for visual interest; mount with yellow eyelets. Write and stamp title words; print and punch letter circles. Wrap blue ribbon across both pages. Layer metal bookplate over date written on yellow cardstock; attach with brads.

Michelle Trunkett, Cape Coral, Florida

Homemade

Words to a lullaby Heather made up while trying to put her newborn to sleep rest in a handmade, stamped and embellished envelope. Journal on vellum; layer under green paper strip. Vertically layer patterned cardstock border. Print title on green cardstock; horizontally layer with cropped matted photo. Mat large photo on green patterned cardstock; mount metal photo corners and attach letter eyelets. Print song lyrics on white cardstock; slip inside stamped and folded envelope. Embellish with buttons and tied raffia.

Heather Melzer, Yorkville, Illinois

Supplies: Patterned paper, envelope design stamp/Anna Griffin; metal letter eyelets, metal photo corners/Making Memories; watermark ink/Tsukineko; green and white cardstocks; vellum; raffia; green buttons

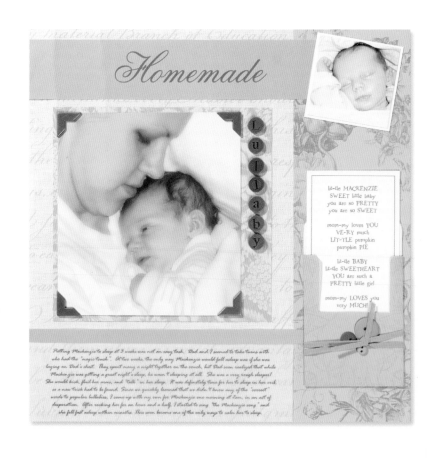

2 in a Tub

Valerie got all her ducks in a row on this clean-cut page. Layer border along top of page with a slice of patterned paper mounted over a slice of blue paper. Slice a wide piece of patterned paper; mount over embossed patterned paper cut to fit bottom half of page. Double mat photo on white and blue papers. Mat geometric design cut from patterned paper on blue paper; mount at left of photo with foam spacers. Assemble a title from stickers and letter beads. Cut paper circles to fit inside metal-rimmed tags; punch hole in one tag and tie with string. Adhere number charm and letter beads on metal-rimmed tags. Mount letter bead on geometric paper design. Adhere stickers for last title word on white cardstock; mat on patterned paper and mount with foam spacers. Draw paper-pieced duck on colored cardstocks; layer pieces, add chalk and pen details. Draw bubble bath bottle on blue vellum and paper; layer pieces, add details. Mount duck next to bottle with foam spacers. Print photo caption on vellum; cut into circle. Adhere transparent bubble stickers around page.

Valerie Salmon, Carmel, Indiana

Supplies: Patterned paper/We R Memory Keepers; letter stickers/Doodlebug Design/Mrs. Grossman's; blue, yellow, red and orange cardstocks; metal-rimmed tag; alphabet beads

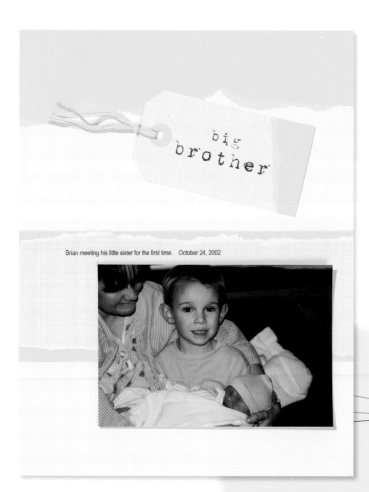

Big Brother

Nikki selected yellow elements for her layout to match her son's yellow shirt against the blue hospital linens in the photo. Layer torn yellow cardstock on white cardstock background. Print title and journaling on yellow patterned cardstock; tear journal strip and layer with yellow cardstock. Cut title into tag; layer with torn yellow cardstock. Punch hole in punched yellow cardstock circle; tie with fibers.

Nikki Pitcher, Olympia, Washington

Supplies: Yellow patterned cardstock/Keeping Memories Alive; yellow and white cardstocks; circle punch; fibers

The Quintessential Squash

Inspired by the colors of fall, Cherie illuminates seasonal photos with the shine of metallic embellishments. Adhere the rich shine of metallic leaf to slide mount frames. Brush liquid adhesive on slide; layer metallic leaf while adhesive is wet and gently press with fingers. Brush off excess leafing; dry. Change the solid color of copper foil sheets by holding over an open flame until colors alter; cool. Do not touch copper to flame. For left page, mat large photo on patterned paper; mount on brown cardstock background. Cut names from patterned paper and orange cardstock; layer at left side of photo. Mount one slide mount over two cropped photos at top of page with foam spacers. Working from top to bottom, assemble the following title elements: embossed word on copper; cut into circle. Attach eyelet and tie with fibers; mount with foam spacers. String silver beads; knot ends. Feed through eyelets attached to page. Cut word from tan cardstock; mat on orange cardstock and silhouette cut. Add chalk and pen details. Layer over circle-punched copper squares attached with eyelets. Emboss letters on small punched circles; layer on larger circles punched from silver foil and mount with foam spacers. Slice a narrow photo strip; cut into four squares and mount under title. Double mat photo on rust cardstock and patterned paper; mount embossed copper photo corners with eyelets. For right page, layer border with strips cut from solid and patterned papers; tear and chalk one edge of each strip. Mount embossed copper squares at top and bottom of border. Starting at top copper square, attach eyelets with fiber in zigzag fashion. Punch squares from photo scraps; mount along border. Journal on vellum; layer over rust cardstock, patterned paper and photo strips. Mount thin patterned paper strip across top of journaling block with brads. Double mat two photos on coordinating solid and patterned papers. Attach eyelets and wrap fibers on diagonal corners of one photo; mount next to journaling. Frame other photo with fibers; string through eyelets attached at corners of second mat. Layer cropped photos behind slides and mount with foam spacers.

Cherie Ward, Colorado Springs, Colorado

Supplies: Patterned paper/Karen Foster Design; letter templates/Chatterbox/Wordsworth; brown, rust, tan and orange cardstocks; vellum; square letter beads; slide mounts; gold leaf; leaf adhesive; fibers; copper sheets; eyelets; brads; square punch; chalk

Same blond hair, same blue eyes…There's no doubt that the two of you are brother and sister. You complete the perfect family – one boy and one girl. You each have your own unique personality and qualities that I love. I can appreciate th[...] jolliness and joy that constantly show in Carlie and the protective- ness and intelligence that Dawson displays. [...] You are both stubborn and headstrong. Dawson is the wild [...]ou who never sleeps and [...]s endless energy while [...]arlie takes naps to recharge. [...] She is the speedy little climber. [...] Nothing stands in her way! She just climbs over it or [...] onto it! Nothing could have prepared me for the task of keeping up with the two of you. You require more energy than I ever knew I had. The things you get into and think up amaze me! I had no idea that I would be so crazy about you both! What a surprise to me that you little guys would take over my whole world! I loved Dawson so much that I never dreamed I could love another child the same way. Once Carlie came along I learned that love grows and I love you both just as fiercely. I can't imagine my life without the two of you!

What an incredible feeling!

I LOVE YOU BOTH SO MUCH

May 2003

.I DIDN'T KNOW IT COULD HAPPEN…

Supplies: Letter stamps/All Night Media; heart nailheads/Westrim; green and black cardstocks; green mulberry paper; sheer ribbon

I Didn't Know It Could Happen…

Dana is surprised to learn how capable she is of unconditionally loving her children as the unique human beings they are. Quadruple mat photo with solid cardstock, torn mulberry and distressed green cardstock with torn edges. Print window border on green cardstock; cut window and mount on black cardstock. Attach sliced green cardstock strips onto distressed photo mat with heart nailheads. "Hang" strips over top of page; offset matted photo from window. Write date on green cardstock strip; mat and mount over ribbon. Journal on green cardstock and mat. Stamp words on green cardstock for title and sentiment. Tear sentiment's edges; crumple, flatten and layer on torn mulberry. Slice word strip; mat and mount over ribbon. Attach heart nailhead.

Dana Swords, Fredericksburg, Virginia

Security in Mama

Sherri's nephew holds tight to the leg of the one who never fails to protect him. Emboss metal word tag and bookplate with gray embossing powder. String word tag with heart charm on layered ribbon; wrap around double-matted photo. Layer with green cardstock on patterned paper background. Die cut letters for title words. Adhere letter pebbles. Mount embossed bookplate over stamped title word with brads. Stamp names.

Sherri Winstead, Fayetteville, North Carolina

Supplies: Patterned paper/K & Co.; letter stamps/Hero Arts; letter pebbles/Li'l Davis Designs; die-cut letters/QuickKutz; metal word tag/(Chronicle Books); metal bookplate/Making Memories; heart charm/www.withcharm.com; green cardstock; ribbon; gray embossing powder; silver brads

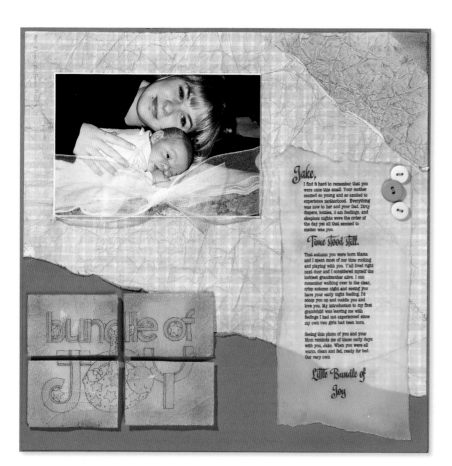

Bundle of Joy

Pam creates the look of fragile cracked glass tiles to represent the delicate essence of life she witnessed during the birth of her grandson. Sand, chalk and slice preprinted title into quarters. Place each section in a "hot pot" skillet and sprinkle with clear extra thick embossing powder; melt. While still warm, sprinkle glass marbles and let cool. Gently crack and reassemble on page. Enhance green cardstock corner as described above. Crumple patterned and solid papers, flatten, iron and chalk. Layer torn corner over distressed patterned paper background; mat on green cardstock. Roll torn edges and mount embossed corner. Diagonally tear green cardstock; layer over bottom left corner of patterned paper and roll edges. Mat photo on white cardstock; wrap and tie sheer ribbon. Journal on vellum; tear and chalk edges. Stitch on buttons with embroidery floss.

Pam Easley, Bentonia, Mississippi

Supplies: Printed paper/Bo-Bunny Press; preprinted title/O'Scrap; green and white cardstocks; vellum; sheer ribbon; embroidery floss; glass marbles; white and green buttons; chalk; sandpaper; extra thick embossing powder

Sweet Child of Mine

Pam embraces the magical bond between female family members with feminine floral patterns, delicate fibers and dimensional flowers. Layer coordinating patterned cardstocks for background; mount torn patterned paper on adjacent corners. Wrap fibers over patterned paper seam. Triple mat photo on solid and patterned cardstocks; stitch second and third mats on page. Print song lyrics on vellum. Silhouette cut flowers from duplicate sheets of patterned paper; layer on page with foam spacers.

Pam Easley, Bentonia, Mississippi

Supplies: Patterned paper and cardstocks/Daisy D's; solid cardstock; vellum; thread; fibers

Sweet Summer Kiss

A tender moment between siblings is a sweet memory for Robin, especially when she finds herself trying to extinguish sibling rivalries! Create background pattern by stamping green cardstock with a lip stamp and watermark ink. Cut to fit half of page; mount on black cardstock. Tear large piece of patterned paper; layer across middle of page. Mount enlarged photo with photo corners. Print title and journaling on vellum; cut and layer on page. Attach title with brads. Mount skeleton leaves near journaling.

Robin Hohenstern, Brooklyn Park, Minnesota

Supplies: Patterned papers/7 Gypsies; stamp/(source unknown); green cardstock; vellum; black brads; skeleton leaves; watermark ink

This is one of my very favorite pictures of Jacob and Claire. It was taken 4th of July weekend in 1999. It was so hot and humid that day that the humidity fogged up the camera lens. I'll always remember how sweetly Jacob treated Claire...until she got older. (just kidding!) He is the best big brother a little girl can hope for!

A Kiss for Daddy

Amy admits that once her baby learned how to show affection, she and her husband couldn't get enough of his sweet kisses. Layer sliced and torn patterned papers over green cardstock. Layer matted photo over fibers vertically mounted along paper seam. Adhere letter stickers on laminate tag. String charm on fibers; wrap and tie on tag. Mount over words printed on inked patterned paper. Attach letter nailheads.

Amy Warren, Tyler, Texas

Supplies: Patterned paper/Keeping Memories Alive/Paper Patch; letter stickers/Colorbök/Creative Imaginations; letter nailheads/ (source unknown); heart charm/(source unknown); laminate tag; green cardstock; fibers

Chapter Openers

Scarlett (page 12)

Create dramatic effects by computer manipulating photo; print and mat on blue cardstock. Stamp green cardstock with tiny hearts and watermark ink. Mount matted photo on green background cardstock with foam spacers. Adhere metal photo corners. Write name and date on metal-rimmed tag; tie with fibers and mount on photo. Print downloaded images from NASA Web site on photo paper; mat on blue cardstock. Print quote on blue vellum; layer over matted photos and adhere metal corners.

Wendy Bickford, Antelope, California

Supplies: Heart stamp/Stampin' Up!; metal photo corners, metal-rimmed tag/Making Memories; blue and green cardstocks; blue vellum; fibers

Trapped in a Baby's Body (page 38)

Mat embossed cardstock on black cardstock for background. Double mat photo on black cardstock and torn patterned paper. Adhere decorative corners. Attach eyelets near bottom of photo; string ribbon with heart charm through eyelets. Create vellum envelope to hold journaling block. Print journaling on ivory cardstock; crop. Ink edges; attach stick pin and slip into envelope. Print title on transparency; cut longer than envelope and attach to page with gold brads secured inside light blue eyelets. Print alphabet on transparency; cut into strips and layer under sheer ribbon. Secure swirl clips to ribbon and page with gold brads.

Denise Tucker, Versailles, Indiana

Supplies: Patterned paper/Anna Griffin; embossed paper/Provo Craft; gold decorative corners, gold stick pin/The Eggery Place; charms/Boutique Trims; swirl clips; black and ivory cardstocks; vellum; transparency; embossing powder; ribbon; gold brads; blue eyelets; metallic rub-ons; ink

Master of His Domain (page 60)

Mimic playhouse design with folded "slats." Slice four 4" strips of tan cardstock; fold over top and bottom edges of strips. Mount on cardstock. Slice a narrow strip of black cardstock; crimp and mount on page. Double mat one photo on black and embossed red cardstocks. Single mat remaining photos with tan and black cardstocks. Layer small photos at bottom of page; ink edges. Punch circles from red and black textured cardstock; layer and journal. Slice a 5⅜" strip of green cardstock and a narrow strip of red embossed cardstock; mount red strip and matted photo on green cardstock. Punch title word in green cardstock strip; outline negative space of letters. Layer title strip over mesh and mat on black textured cardstock. Journal on tan cardstock; cut and mount at bottom of page under title strip. Stamp first title word letters on brown cardstock circles; mount on silver-rimmed tags. Press lettered tag onto watermark ink pad and sprinkle with extra thick embossing powder; heat to set; repeat and mount. Write balance of title words with white correction pen.

Michelle Pendleton, Colorado Springs, Colorado

Supplies: Embossed paper/(source unknown); letter stamps/Stamp Craft; tan, black, green and red cardstocks; silver-rimmed tags; extra thick embossing powder; paper crimper; circle punch; mesh; correction pen

The Whole World (page 82)

Paint edges of cream cardstock with gold powdered paint mixed with a gel medium. Mat photos on torn brown textured paper; mount on page with eyelets. Print title and journaling on vellum; tear and chalk edges. Mount with brads. Adhere letter stickers to journaling block; embellish tag letters with brads. Cut circle and square tags from ivory cardstock; punch hole. Chalk tag edges; outline with brown marker. Adhere toy stickers to crumpled and flattened ivory cardstock scraps; tear and chalk edges before mounting on tags. Tie with fibers. Clip tag to vellum journaling block with swirl clip.

Anne Louise Rigsby, Cottonwood, Arizona

Supplies: Textured paper/Emagination Crafts; letter stickers/EK Success; stickers/Mrs. Grossman's; fibers; brads; gold paint; gel medium; chalk; swirl clip

Loving Ian (page 104)

Create border at top of page with narrow strip of patterned paper and very narrow strip of blue cardstock layered on a green cardstock background. For bottom border, layer a strip of patterned paper over a strip of blue cardstock and a strip of torn blue patterned paper. Stamp vertical title word; print large title word on black cardstock and silhouette cut. Double mat photo on black and blue cardstocks; mount photo corners. Cut a rectangular piece of blue paper; stitch along border. Create envelope from green vellum. Loop metal-rimmed tag on patterned paper strip and mount along bottom of envelope. Wrap ribbon around envelope; secure with adhesive poem stone. Slip photo inside envelope and mount on stitched blue strip; mount. Journal on tag; stamp date. Mount preprinted tag at top of blue strip with foam spacers. Print poem on vellum; mount patterned paper strip, layer on page and affix letter bead as first letter of poem. Mount cropped photo behind blue preprinted slide frame; wrap with wire and mount with foam spacers.

Valerie Salmon, Carmel, Indiana
Poem: Susan Schiltz

Supplies: Patterned paper, preprinted tag, preprinted slide mount/KI Memories; letter stamps/Hero Arts; letter bead/Westrim; silver photo corners; poem stone Creative Imaginations; blue, black and green cardstocks; blue paper; vellum; metal-rimmed tag; ribbon; wire

Sources

The following companies manufacture products showcased on scrapbook pages within this book. Please check your local retailers to find these materials. We have made every attempt to properly credit the items mentioned in this book and apologize to those we may have missed.

2DYE4
(519) 537-6756
www.canscrapink.com

3M Stationary
(800) 364-3577
www.3M.com

7 Gypsies
(800) 588-6707
www.7gypsies.com

Accent Depot
(630) 548-2133
www.accentdepot.com

All My Memories
(888) 553-1998
www.allmymemories.com

All Night Media (see Plaid Enterprises)

American Art Clay Company
(AMACO)
(800) 374-1600
www.amaco.com

American Tag Company
(800) 223-3956
www.americantag.net

Amscan, Inc.
(800) 444-8887
www.amscan.com

Anima Designs
(800) 570-6847
www.animadesigns.com

Anna Griffin, Inc (wholesale only)
(888) 817-8170
www.annagriffin.com

Avery
(800) G0-AVERY
www.avery.com

Bazzill Basics Paper
(480) 558-8557
www.bazzillbasics.com

Bo-Bunny Press
(801) 771-0481
www.bobunny.com

Books By Hand & Solum World
(505) 255-3534

Boutique Trims, Inc.
(248) 437-2017
www.boutiquetrims.com

Boxer Scrapbook Productions
(503) 625-0455
www.boxerscrapbooks.com

Canada Scrapbooks!–no contact info. available

Card Connection, The
www.michaels.com

Carolee's Creations®
(435) 563-1100
www.carolees.com

Charming Pages
(888) 889-5060

Chatterbox, Inc.
(208) 939-9133
www.chatterboxinc.com

Chronicle Books
www.chroniclebooks.com

Close To My Heart®
(888) 655-6552
www.closetomyheart.com

Club Scrap™
(888) 634-9100
www.clubscrap.com

Colorbök™, Inc. (wholesale only)
(800) 366-4660
www.colorbok.com

Colors By Design
(800) 832-8436
www.colorsbydesign.com

Composite Crafts–no contact info. available

Craft Print– no contact info available

Crafts, Etc. Ltd.
www.craftsetc.com

Creative Imaginations (wholesale only)
(800) 942-6487
www.cigift.com

C-Thru® Ruler Company, The
(wholesale only)
(800) 243-8419
www.cthruruler.com

Cut-It-Up™
(530) 389-2233
www.cut-it-up.com

Daisy D's Paper Company
(888) 601-8955
www.daisydspaper.com

Darice, Inc.
(800) 321-1494
www.darice.com

Deluxe Designs
(480) 497-9005
www.deluxecuts.com

DeNami Design
(253) 437-1626
www.denamidesign.com

Design Originals
(800) 877-7820
www.d-originals.com

DMD Industries, Inc. (wholesale only)
(800) 805-9890
www.dmdind.com

Doodlebug Design Inc.™
(801) 966-9952

Dymo
www.dymo.com

Eggery Place, The
www.theeggeryplace.com

EK Success™, Ltd. (wholesale only)
(800) 524-1349
www.eksuccess.com

Emagination Crafts, Inc.
(wholesale only)
(630) 833-9521
www.emaginationcrafts.com

Family Treasures, Inc.®
www.familytreasures.com

Fiskars, Inc. (wholesale only)
(715) 842-2091
www.fiskars.com

Foofala
(402) 330-3208
www.foofala.com

Frances Meyer, Inc.®
(800) 372-6237
www.francesmeyer.com

Georgia Bonesteel
www.georgiabonesteel.com

Gifted Line, The
(800) 533-7263

Handmade Creations–no contact info avaialble

Heartland Crafts–no contact info available

Heidi Grace Designs
(866) 89-heidi
www.heidigrace.com

Hero Arts® Rubber Stamps, Inc.
(wholesale only)
(800) 822-4376
www.heroarts.com

Hirschberg, Schutz & Co., Inc.
(800) 221-8640

Honey Cottage–no contact info available

Hot Off The Press, Inc.
(800) 227-9595
www.paperpizazz.com

Hot Potatoes
(615) 269-8002
www.hotpotatoes.com

Inkadinkado® Rubber Stamps
(800) 888-4652
www.inkadinkado.com

It Takes Two®
(800) 331-9843
www.ittakestwo.com

Jennifer Collection, The
(518) 272-4572

Jesse James & Co., Inc.
(610) 435-0201
www.jessejamesbutton.com

Jest Charming
(702) 564-5101
www.jestcharming.com

JudiKins
(310) 515-1115
www.judikins.com

K & Company
(888) 244-2083
www.kandcompany.com

Karen Foster Design™ (wholesale only)
(801) 451-9779
www.karenfosterdesign.com

KI Memories
www.kimemories.com

Kopp Design
(208) 656-0734
www.koppdesign.com

Lasting Impressions for Paper, Inc.
(801) 298-1979
www.lastingimpressions.com

Leeco Industries, Inc.
(800) 826-8806
www.leecoindustries.com

Li'l Davis Designs
(949) 838-0344
www.lildavisdesigns.com

Magenta Rubber Stamps
(wholesale only)
(800) 565-5254
www.magentarubberstamps.com

Magic Mesh™
(651) 345-6374
www.magicmesh.com

Magic Scraps™
(972) 238-1838
www.magicscraps.com

Making Memories
(800) 286-5263
www.makingmemories.com

Me & My Big Ideas (wholesale only)
(949) 589-4607
www.meandmybigideas.com

Ma Vinci's Reliquary
www.crafts.dm.net

Memories Complete™, LLC
(866) 966-6365
www.memoriescomplete.com

Mrs. Grossman's Paper Co.
(wholesale only)
(800) 429-4549
www.mrsgrossmans.com

Mustard Moon™
(408) 229-8542
www.mustardmoon.com

My Mind's Eye™, Inc.
(801) 298-3709
www.frame-ups.com

Office Depot
www.officedepot.com

Okie-Dokie Press, The
(801) 298-1028

O'Scrap!/Imaginations, Inc.
(801) 225-6015
www.imaginations-inc.com

Paper Adventures® (wholesale only)
(800) 727-0699
www.paperadventures.com

Paper House Productions
(800) 255-7316
www.paperhouseproductions.com

Paper Patch®, The
(800) 397-2737
www.paperpatch.com

Patchwork Paper Design
(480) 515-0537
www.patchworkpaper.com

Pebbles, Inc.
(800) 438-8153
www.pebblesinc.com

Penny Black Inc.
(510) 849-1883
www.pennyblackinc.com

Pioneer Photo Albums, Inc.®
(800) 366-3686
www.pioneerphotoalbums.com

Plaid Enterprises, Inc.
(800) 842-4197
www.plaidonline.com

Precious Accents–no contact info available

PrintWorks
(800) 854-6558
www.printworkscollection.com

Provo Craft® (wholesale only)
(888) 577-3545
www.provocraft.com

PSX Design™
(800) 782-6748
www.psxdesign.com

Pulsar Paper Products
(877) 861-0031
www.pulsarpaper.com

QuicKutz®
(888) 702-1146
www.quickutz.com

Rhode Island Bead and Components
(401) 464-4411
www.RIBead.com

Robert Schumann–no contact info available

Robin's Nest Press, The
(wholesale only)
(435) 789-5387
www.robinsnest-scrapbook.com

Rubber Stampede
(800) 423-4135
www.rubberstampede.com

Rusty Pickle
(801) 272-2280
www.rustypickle.com

Sam Moon Trading Co.
www.sammoongroup.com

ScrapArts
(503) 631-4893
www.scraparts.com

Scrap Pagerz
(435) 645-0696
www.scrappagerz.com

Scrapworks, LLC
www.scrapworksllc.com

SEI, Inc.
(800) 333-3279
www.shopsei.com

Simply Charmed–no contact info available

Sonburn, Inc. (wholesale only)
(800) 527-7505
www.theroyalstore.com

Staedtler®, Inc.
(800) 927-7723
www.staedtler-usa.com

Stampa Rosa–no longer in business

Stamp Craft–(see Plaid Enterprises)

Stamp Doctor, The
www.stampdoctor.com

Stampendous!®
(800) 869-0474
www.stampendous.com

Stamp in the Hand, A
(310) 884-9700
www.astampinthehand.com

Stampin' Up!®
(800) 782-6787
www.stampinup.com

Sweetwater
(800) 359-3094
www.sweetwaterscrapbook.com

Tsukineko®, Inc.
(800) 769-6633
www.tsukineko.com

We R Memory Keepers
(801) 539-5000
www.weronthenet.com

Westrim® Crafts
(800) 727-2727
www.westrimcrafts.com

With Charm–no contact info available

Wordsworth
(719) 282-3495
www.wordsworthstamps.com

Worldwin
(608) 834-9900
www.thepapermill.com

Wübie Prints
(888) 256-0107
www.wubieprints.com

Index

A

Additional instructions, 126

B

Baby trivia, 66

The best gift my child received, 30, 33

C

Calendar journaling, 72

Colors and black-and-white photos, 92

Computer-generated images, 27, 33

Creating a scrapbook page, 10

Creative quotes, 117

D

Display of documents, 20

Documenting baby's growth, 70

G

Garage photo studio, 51

Get really close, 50

Getting that perfect baby portrait, 49

Great close-up photos, 48

Growth chart, 23, 71

H

Hidden journaling, 26, 89, 90

I

If I could scrapbook about just one of my child's traits, 52

Including memorabilia on your pages, 94

Index, 128

Introduction, 6

J

Journaling about baby, 119

L

Let's Shoot Some Black-and-White, 82-103

Lights, Camera, ACTION!, 60-81

M

Mosaic, 76

Move in for a Close-Up, 38-59

Memorabilia checklist, 16

Most popular baby names in 1902, 25

Most popular baby names in 2002, 27

My baby taught me, 67, 75, 78

P

Pop art, 52

S

Set up a garage photo studio, 51

Shooting better black-and-white photos, 84

Sources, 127

A Star Is Born, 12-37

The Supporting Cast, 104-125

T

Table of Contents, 4

Take better action shots, 62

Title ideas for pages starring baby, 116

Tools and supplies, 4

U

Ultrasound photos, 14

V

Vintage photo, 57